Giving My All

Giving My All

An Autobiography

Earl Martin Phalen

NEW YORK

LONDON • NASHVILLE • MELBOURNE • VANCOUVER

Giving My All

The Autobiography of Earl Martin Phalen

Published in New York, New York, by Morgan James Publishing. Morgan James is a trademark of Morgan James, LLC. www.MorganJamesPublishing.com

Proudly distributed by Publishers Group West®

ISBN 9781636980508 paperback
ISBN 9781636980515 ebook
Library of Congress Control Number:
2022945263

Cover and Interior Design by:
Chris Treccani
www.3dogcreative.net

Morgan James is a proud partner of Habitat for Humanity Peninsula and Greater Williamsburg. Partners in building since 2006.

Get involved today! Visit: www.morgan-james-publishing.com/giving-back

TABLE OF CONTENTS

ACKNOWLEDGEMENTS

My family, friends, and colleagues are my greatest gifts in life. Without your love and support, I would have no story to tell. Without your talents, friendship, and guidance, there would have been no dream to pursue.

To my mom and dad, your unconditional love still carries me. The strong example that you set throughout my life is the reason I have been blessed to have an impact in the world, and none of what I have been able to accomplish would have been possible or realized without you. To my siblings, Mary, Jimmy, Ann, Joan, Patty, David, and Steve you have provided love, support, voices of reason, support for my "crazy" ideas, and warnings about what potholes might lie in the road ahead so that I can avoid. Beyond Mom and Dad, you have been the greatest influences in making me who I am, less my faults which I fully own. Thank you.

To my friends who have been there with me through so much—my highest highs and my lowest lows—thank you for always being there for and with me. My evolution would not have happened without the consistency of your friendship, perspective, encouragement, direction, and love. Thank you, as well, to all who believed in and participated in serving our scholars over the past three decades—you have been and are a consistent source of inspiration for me. Seeing the impact that we have had and are having, and the daily work you do for our scholars, gives me hope.

I would also like to thank the people along the way who doubted us, who didn't believe in me. You sparked a fire that drove me forward, and I am deeply grateful for that and for you.

Again, though, to my teammates, your partnership, your passion, your sheer belief in the work, and your commitment to our community is evident in every thread of the fabric of what has become the George and Veronica Phalen Leadership Academies. Thank you for believing we can change the lives of children across the country, and for doing it each and every day. This story is my story, your story, and the story of my family, friends, teachers, coaches, and mentors. Thank you.

The stories in this book reflect my memories and recollections. Some names, locations, and identifying characteristics have been changed to protect the privacy of individuals. Dialogue has been re-created from memory.

Missing the Shot

Thirteen seconds left on the clock. Packed bleachers on both sides of the basketball court. The Norwood High School Mustangs were playing our rivals, the Wellesley High School Raiders. We'd been sluggish in the first half, and Wellesley had surged ahead. After halftime we rallied for fifteen grueling minutes, a hard-fought comeback. Now, we were just one point behind.

Coach Johnson called a timeout and got us in a huddle.

"All right, all right," he said. "Kenny, you inbound the ball to David, and let's get a hard back screen for Ned."

Ned was our star, Coach Johnson's favorite.

"Ned," Coach said, "you take the shot."

With a shout of "Teamwork!" we ran back onto the court, ready to save the day. But things didn't go as planned. Wellesley's defense was on top of us. Kenny couldn't get a clean pass and threw wildly to avoid a five-second violation. David, with his long skinny arms, managed to get the ball, but he was stuck behind Wellesley's two best defenders.

"DEFENSE!" The Wellesley bleachers were going wild. We had to do something.

I executed a pick-and-roll, just like Coach had taught us. I got open on the left and David managed to muscle a pass through to me. Five seconds left. I had a great shot, an open look from the foul line.

And I froze.

"SHOOT! SHOOT!" The Mustang bleachers cheered me on.

But I couldn't shoot. It couldn't be me. This was supposed to be Ned's winning shot. Where was Ned?

Three seconds. Ned was swarmed by two defenders. Two seconds. I made a panicked pass that Ned just managed to reach. One second. With no clear shot, Ned heaved the ball into the air.

The buzzer rang. The ball hit the side of the backboard. We had lost.

Wild yells erupted from Wellesley as the crowd poured onto the court, but I was stuck in silence. The last thirteen seconds kept replaying in my mind. I could have had the winning shot. Why had I choked?

Back in the locker room, Coach Johnson yelled at us until his face turned red. I knew when he pointed and inadvertently spat and said that "we" all blew it, he was really talking about me. But I also knew he had never wanted me to save the day. Ned, with his tall height, athleticism, and easy, unshakable confidence, would never have hesitated. He was supposed to be the hero, not me. It had been my ball, but it wasn't my shot.

I wish I could say that at the next Mustang game, I stepped up and led the team to victory. It didn't happen that way. Coach Johnson never warmed to me or gave me credit for my skills, but it wasn't all his fault that I underperformed that season. I've revisited that day on the court many times over the years. It wasn't the first or the last time I came close to fulfilling my potential, only to hold myself back. I can still hear the loud voices urging me to take the shot, the yells from the crowd and the cheers from my buddies on the bench. But there are still those softer, more insistent voices, the ones warning me to stay out of the spotlight. Much of my life has been a struggle against those voices, a struggle to let myself win.

CHAPTER 1

Where I Come From

Meeting My Family

L ife has a way of surprising you with big decisions. I had to make my first one when I was just two years old. I was born on February 10, 1967, in Springfield, Massachusetts. My birth mother was just eighteen years old, away from her family and unprepared to be a mom. We had half an hour together, and then the nurses took me away. My first years were spent in one foster home, then another. I'm told I was a favorite at my second place, a smart, talkative toddler who was already toilet trained. Still, it wasn't easy being one of twelve kids, in a home that wouldn't be mine forever. By age two, I knew how to charm adults and how to fight off other kids—my mom told me once that one of the first things I said to my brother David was "get your f**king hands off my food." A pretty sophisticated threat for a toddler, one I must have had to make before. I was a precocious child—I had to be.

I had been living at my second foster home for just under a year the day my social worker Fran picked me up and took me out for strawberry ice cream—my favorite. We went to play in the park, and there was a couple there, a man and a woman. Fran, the couple, and I played for a few hours, tossing a ball around. The man and the woman took me to a cart and bought me a hot dog—my other favorite. When it was time to go home, Fran asked me if I had liked the couple we met. I must have said yes, because the next day we saw them again. Fran left for a while and the couple, Mr. and Mrs. Phalen, took care of me, playing those simple games that toddlers can't get enough of. At the end of the day, Fran asked me an important question.

"Would you like Mr. and Mrs. Phalen to be your new mommy and daddy?"

I looked at her and said yes. And that was that.

That night, I packed a little bag with all my clothes inside. I carried it to my parents' car all by myself. Fran hugged me goodbye and promised to visit me the next weekend. My mom told me I was very sad that first night in my new home. I don't remember those early days, but I think I must have been lonely, knowing I had said good-bye to all the people who had loved me up until then. I had taken a huge leap of faith for such a small child. But the next morning, I woke up to my new life: the baby brother of eight kids in a warm, energetic, loving family. I was a Phalen.

It's strange to think that I ever chose my parents. They are so much a part of who I am. Whenever I work nights crunching numbers or drafting a proposal, I see reflections of my father, steady, hardworking, and judicious. How would I have found a career working with children if I had never soaked up my mom's strength and patience, her joy and love for all? But maybe it's not so strange that my parents and I belonged together. They chose me just as much as I chose them.

George and Veronica Phalen

My parents' choice was decades in the making. The year they adopted me, 1969, George and Veronica Phalen were in their forties, married for over twenty years and the parents of seven children. The two of them had already lived through some of the biggest changes in American history. My mom was born in Norwood, Massachusetts.

Her father had emigrated from Ireland as a young man. He built a good life for his family, but he never forgot his struggles to find a foothold in America, looking for jobs and reading Irish Need Not Apply in the storefront windows. My mom inherited his independent spirit and his love of justice. She admitted to me once that she had only started one fight in her whole life. My mom was always a fantastic athlete, a sprinter who could outrun her whole grade. One day, our national women's soccer team came to her elementary school to talk to the kids. The captain gave my mom a soccer ball, a fantastic treasure in her eyes. One of the boys in her class tried to steal it, and she punched him! My mom came from a devout and upright family, but her dad didn't give her any trouble about the fight. I think he liked having a daughter who could stick up for herself.

My dad grew up just a few neighborhoods over, in a part of Norwood called "Swedesville." Neither of my parents were the type of people to complain or dwell on the past. Still, they were both Great Depression kids from modest families, and I know those tough and uncertain years left their mark. We kids grew up comfortable, but my mom never gave up clipping coupons every week. Leftover Night was a family institution, since both my parents thought that wasting food was almost a sin. My dad, practical to the core, never understood why people spent money on flashy stuff like designer clothes. Growing up, I watched my mom pick his outfits for him, just so he didn't go to work with a mismatched tie and different shoes on each foot.

My parents fell in love in high school and married young, just in time for the postwar baby boom. In those days, the Roman Catholic Church made its message clear: children were a blessing, and Catholic families should have as many blessings as they possibly could. My sister Mary came first, then Jimmy, Ann, Joan, Patty, and David. Mom and Dad had always hoped for ten kids, but my brother Steve's birth was dangerous and difficult. He and my mom almost didn't make it, and doctors warned her not to try for another child.

As their family grew, my parents had happy, prosperous years. After college, my dad started his career as an entry-level banker, a loan officer trainee; through talent and steady hard work, he climbed the ladder and became the vice chairman at the First National Bank of Boston. He always had a good head for business, but what struck me most growing up was his unflagging self-discipline. He worked all day and a few hours each evening, although he always made time for family dinner, and for each of us.

And even though my dad dealt with great wealth, he never compromised his values. My brother David once told me the story of a business trip he took with my dad, back when my dad ran Bank of Boston's Latin America division. They met with a crisply dressed businessman from a South American city who told my dad that if he wanted to get ahead in that town, he would have to get used to giving bribes. My dad refused.

The businessman waved it off as a local custom: "When in Rome," he said, "do as the Romans do."

"I may be in Rome," my dad replied, "but I'm going to do as the Bostonians do." He didn't give an inch, and as it turns out, he didn't have to. He made the division a success, doing business his own way.

My dad had the kind of integrity that commanded respect. His faith in his own judgment helped him take risks and find paths others couldn't see. His biggest dream was to build something lasting for our family. In the 1950s, my mom and dad decided that the Phalens needed their own summer place. My dad had his eye on Duxbury, Massachusetts, a quaint town near Cape Cod. All of my dad's buddies wanted a Duxbury beachfront property, with bragging rights to a view of the Bay. My dad saw things differently. He got a great deal on fifty acres a little ways away from the beach. He saved on taxes by turning much of the property into a tree farm, and the growth began. My dad established a house for our family, and he built two more over the years. He lived to see his grandchildren driving around the Phalen family land, the place we all gather every summer.

My mom was just as strong-minded as my dad was. The two of them were so similar that way, so alike in their individuality. They made a great team. My calm, introverted dad loved the way my mom could talk to just about anyone. Strangers loved her immediately, and she usually loved them right back. The worst thing I ever heard her say about people was that they weren't "my cup of tea." Very few earned even that much criticism; people in general were her cup of tea. Our house was the neighborhood house, and sometimes it felt like she was everyone's mom.

My parents were people of faith. We grew up going to Mass every Sunday—daily during Lent. My mother's favorite parable was the story of the Good Samaritan. To her, faith in God meant loving others, and loving others meant helping and protecting them. My mother loved Jesus, and she respected the Church, but rote obedience was never her thing. She disagreed with many Church traditions, including the limited roles available to women, and she didn't hesitate to speak her mind. In the 1980s, my mom first learned of the Church's role in protecting sexually abusive priests. Heartbroken, she wrote a letter to our cardinal, urging him to take stronger action. Later, when she realized the true extent of the abuse and the cover-up, my mom walked away. She left the Church she was born into, and she never looked back, because protecting children came first. She never lost her faith in God, but she found Him out in the world, in the way she showed up for people.

My Parents' Decision

The 1960s were a time of tremendous change. When my parents were young, breaking news came through the evening paper, maybe a radio broadcast if you were lucky enough to catch it. By 1960, over three-fourths of Americans had a TV set in their homes. For the first time, the news was live and on film, night after night. It was a small revolution. And it helped ignite a bigger one. All across the country, Black Americans were fighting to claim the fundamental rights they had been denied for so long. When Martin Luther King Jr. led the 1963 March on Washington, hundreds of thousands of people filled the National Mall, listening in awe to "I Have a Dream." And his words echoed, in real time, into millions of homes, across the country and across the world. My mom watched the news every night and saw young men and women braving police dogs, batons, and hoses, united in the pursuit of justice. She couldn't look away. And she didn't want to.

My mom told my dad that she wanted to go with the Freedom Riders on the bus to Alabama, to join in the fight for civil rights. He told her it would never work. They had seven kids at home! My dad's cautious, analytical nature couldn't abide it. My mom's heart was telling her that she couldn't stand idly by. She stayed in Massachusetts, but she felt restless, like her work was unfinished. One day, my mom picked up the *Boston Globe* and read something that stopped her in her tracks. Of all the Black boys born into Massachusetts foster care, the *Globe* reported, 70 percent would end up in the prison system by age twenty-one. My mom felt the call then, more clearly. She and my dad could share the greatest gift they had: their family. They would become parents to a young Black boy.

Always a team, my parents wasted no time. My dad sat dutifully through their state-mandated parenting classes, although I'm sure he wanted to roll his eyes and get back home to his seven kids. My mom hoped for a newborn baby, but when their social worker asked my parents to consider an older child, she listened and committed to keeping an open mind. When Fran matched my parents with me, my mom and dad were ready. We were ready for each other.

My Legacy, My History

Growing up, I knew all about how I had started my life with my family. But I was an adult before I learned the real story of the day I was born. There was someone else in the room with my birth mother, Mary Ann, and me that day: my birth father's mother, my grandmom Canaday McQueen. When my grandmom found out that her son was expecting a child, she wanted to raise me herself. Her husband wouldn't agree to it. My grandmom finally accepted the adoption, but she made up her mind that at the very least, she would get to see me. She traveled from her home in North Carolina to Massachusetts to support my birth mother through her labor. My grandmom was the one who pleaded with the nurses, convincing them to let the three of us have just thirty minutes together, huddled around that hospital bed. Back then, birth relatives usually got no time with the baby at all. I was thirty-five when my grandmom, filled with joy at seeing me again, told me the story of the first time we met. She had never forgotten

February 10, she said: she celebrated my birthday all those years, knowing I was out there somewhere.

When I met my grandmom again, I looked for my own features in her face, her warm eyes and confident smile. I was struck by how much she reminded me of my mom. The same kindness, the same protectiveness, the same strength. She was faithful like my mom, a natural leader. After she and her husband divorced, Grandmom became the president of her local NAACP chapter, at a time when women rarely got leadership roles. But for my grandmom, breaking that kind of ground was barely noteworthy. She simply did what had to be done.

My grandmom had grown up in small-town North Carolina, in a large, closely knit extended family. Her own grandfather had been a larger-than-life man, a Baptist preacher who stood seven feet tall and fathered eighteen children. My great-great-grandfather grew up in very difficult times. He had come of age in the years just after the end of the Civil War and taken a long, hard look at the world around him. He understood that many of the white people of defeated North Carolina would do anything they could to keep free Black families from thriving. Black customers had to pay prices that were twice, five times what white people paid, at stores that made them come in through the back door. The threat of violence was thick in the air, especially for Black people who dared to succeed. So, he found another way. My great-great-grandfather used the tithes from his congregation to open his own store, then another, then another. With his profits from the stores, he invested in land until his holdings grew to over 600 acres. My grandmom lived on the family land, carrying on the legacy he left.

I once asked Grandmom what it had been like, growing up in a mixed community, living through segregation and integration. She told me it had been great. Great, I wondered, learning to get along with all types of people?

Her eyes flashed.

"Great because it taught you about an eye for an eye," she said, holding my gaze. "If the white man does something to you, you come back twice as hard, so he knows never to mess with you again." Grandmom told me about a time her husband was away on business. My birth father and my uncle, two school-aged kids, went into town to run an errand at the store. After they left, a rumor spread that the two of them had disrespected a white woman there. Maybe they had spoken to this woman or looked her in the eye. Maybe they had done nothing at all. The Ku Klux Klan showed up at my grandmom's house that night, demanding she bring the boys outside. My grandmom, cool and calm, told her sons to take cover and gathered her shotguns. With a loaded gun in her hands, she told the mob that if they ever stepped foot on her property again, it would be the last thing they ever did. There would be war, and she would not lose. The KKK never went near her children again.

Grandmom looked at me, and this time she smiled. "This is your history, son," she said.

I've often wondered what my life would have been like if I'd grown up with that deep sense of Black pride, of the right to self-determination. My grandmom reminded me that it's been inside me all along. My history.

Earl Martin Phalen

In our half hour together, my birth mother named me Earl Wayne Canaday McQueen. When I became a Phalen, my mom gave me the middle name Martin, in honor of Dr. Martin Luther King Jr. It's a name of great expectations, a name to be lived up to. I don't take any of those names lightly. Earl, the person I have always been, Martin, the kind of person I can strive to be, and Phalen, the family I chose and the family that shaped me.

It's never just Earl Phalen.

I am Earl Martin Phalen.

CHAPTER 2

Growing Up

Family Dinner

My mom made the kitchen the center of our home; every evening, she would get to work, and the house would fill up with the smell of chicken and rice, juicy rib eyes, lasagna, and fresh, warm bread. With the call of "dinner's ready," we all started showing up at the table. My mom would put out a small feast, complete with roasted vegetables and a big salad. She was the family chef, and my dad always made it home in time for dinner. Our friends were welcome; later, my sisters' boyfriends joined, then their husbands and their kids. There was a cheerful cacophony of voices, talking over each other, arguing about the game and who'd taken too many mashed potatoes. I had to eat quickly, especially when David and Steve were around, because it all went fast. Nothing was taboo, and no one talked down to the kids. I would pick things up by osmosis. There was a place called Palestine, and a place called Israel, and they didn't get along. The peace process had stalled, meetings were tense, and what did I think the president should do next?

My dad could be a man of few words—often firm, decisive ones. But I never felt intimidated by his reserve, and I liked that he spoke carefully. My mom had once aspired to write for *Time* magazine, and our family was her journalistic roundtable. No topic was off-limits. She and my dad would hear out each of their contributors, with patience and respect. It was my first lesson in learning how to claim my time and defend my point of view. No wonder a few of us became lawyers.

When I think of my parents' love in action, I think about those nights around the kitchen table. Every child deserves that kind of nourishment, a place to be fed and a place to be heard.

Big Brothers and Sisters

Being the baby brother has its perks. Seven role models, seven protectors. My sister Mary was twenty years older than I was, and even Steve, who was the second youngest, had five years on me. Our family was so big that we eventually had to come up with a system for Christmas gifts; each person purchased a gift for one sibling and got a gift from one sibling. Except for the loophole: me. I got presents from everybody until I was halfway through college.

My oldest siblings were almost out of the house when I was adopted. As I grew up, they moved out, to college, Boston, families of their own. When they did come back home, everything felt more exciting. I can still remember my brother Jimmy pulling up on his motorcycle, ready to take us all out for a ride around the neighborhood or to go get fried clams near the beach. He seemed larger-than-life, with his generous laugh and freewheeling spirit. Jimmy has been a touchstone for me throughout my career. Though he was never able to focus in school and was an average student, he had a brilliant career in finance, and like my dad, he has an irritating knack for being always right about matters of business. I haven't always followed his advice, but I've always been lucky to count on his support. After Phalen Leadership Academies had been running an elementary school in Indianapolis for a few years, I decided it was the time to expand. Jimmy told me he thought I was taking on too much, too soon. He told me not to plan for a middle school and high school when we were still struggling with K-6 enrollment. He was right, from a business perspective. But it was a risk I knew I had to take. In the end, Jimmy shook his head and he and my sister-in-law Rosemary helped us make it happen. Today, the James and Rosemary Phalen Academy in Indianapolis serves over 700 scholars in grades 7-12.

But it was my brother David, nine years my senior and living at home through law school, who was the sibling I looked up to most when I was young. He looked so cool to me when I was a little kid, with his big, welcoming laugh and dirty blond hair. He understood me, and he was gentle with me. I turned to David whenever I was struggling, whenever I felt afraid. And he always had a lot of advice and guidance to share.

The Sea and the High Road

The truth is, I was often afraid as a child. My childhood had a lot of joy, mixed with a lot of fear. In the summers we would go out to the Duxbury house and spend all day at the beach. I was a sandcastle expert, making elaborate quadruple-moated fortresses that could stay up overnight. When we got home from the water, my sister Joanie would get some oil and a pick and comb out my hair, getting the sand out from my roots. I felt so calm in those moments, and so loved.

But I never really liked being in the water. When I was just a toddler, I was splashing on the shoreline with my mom, and I got sucked under by a wave. My mom, frantic, pulled me back out, throwing out her elbow in the process. It never really healed, and I never forgot the suddenness of that fear and the shock of the cold. You can never be totally sure of yourself in the ocean. Even the strongest swimmers are no match for the power of the undertow. David, who was usually so patient with me, never quite understood why I didn't want to go waterskiing. I couldn't explain it back then, but it was something about the deep, shifting force of the water, making you feel totally surrounded and totally alone at the same time. I understood that feeling, more than I wanted to.

One ordinary day, I was walking through town with my sisters. A car filled with a group of laughing teenagers made a wide, clumsy U-turn. One of the kids rolled down the window as they passed us by.

"You ni**er lovers!" he screamed, and the laughter got louder as the car sped away.

My sisters were hot with anger. "Those idiots" Patty hissed. "Did you see the license plate?" Joanie pulled me aside and asked if I was OK. Of course, I said yes. Even if I wasn't OK, I felt protected by the look of concern in her eyes, the disgust on my sisters' faces.

When strangers would insult me, my siblings wanted to join up and fight back. My parents always held firm: we would do nothing of the sort.

"There are a lot of ignorant people out there, Earl," my mom would say to me.

"Some people can't change," my father would explain. "You can't respond to hate with hate."

My mom and dad's faith taught them that it was best to rise above insults, to turn the other cheek. My parents practiced what they preached. They lost colleagues after they adopted me, and some doors closed to them socially. When one of the country clubs in Duxbury rejected them for having a Black child, they simply accepted the decision and applied to another one. If they had any bitterness about the people and things they lost, they refused to let it show.

All of these years later, I understand where my mom and dad were coming from. I've had a lot of time to come to terms with the way some people will always see me. I refuse to let someone else's ignorance disturb my peace or keep me from what I want.

But a child can't really be the bigger person. How can a scrawny kid be bigger than six teenagers in a car? All kids know is that they need other people's acceptance just to survive. I couldn't fight everyone. Trying would have just worn me out. The current was much too strong. So I made a decision early on: I would fit in instead.

I took care not to stand out. I avoided any talk of race, ran away from suggestions that I could be different from my siblings or the kids in my grade. My mom would try now and then to have our family discuss race, and to help me take pride in my heritage. She had us all watch *Roots* together, wanted us to talk about its lessons. I wasn't having it. Good, bad, proud, ashamed—it didn't matter. I just didn't want to be different.

I don't think everyone saw that sensitive, fearful side of me as a kid. At home, I cried easily and I was sometimes anxious. A small change in my mom's tone of voice could set me off. At school, I was fun and upbeat, the kid in the back row who makes jokes that even the teacher laughs at. I remember the elementary school teachers would let me and my friend Robbie do our lessons standing up, just to get some of our goofy, upbeat energy out. I made friends easily, and the girls in my elementary school yearbook all told me I was a flirt. I was fun to be with, and I had a lot of fun, but there were many things I let slide, moments I knew no one else really understood. They didn't see me working to tread water.

Calling Cheryl

The stakes are so high in adolescence. Every social interaction feels like a tremendous gamble, just one wrong move away from social annihilation. In sixth grade, I had the biggest crush on my friend Cheryl. She was a tall tomboy with dirty blonde hair—my dream girl. We used to play kickball together after school, and she laughed at all my jokes. I told my friend Matt about my crush and he agreed—Cheryl totally liked me. All I had to do was muster up the courage and ask her out.

I went over to Matt's house, and we pulled up two chairs by his landline. I forced myself to pick up the phone and dial her number. One ring, two rings, and I heard her voice on the other line.

"Hi, Cheryl," I said, willing my voice not to break. "It's me, Earl."

"Oh…hey Earl," she said, a little hesitantly. "How are you?"

"I'm, I'm good…it was really good to hang out today after school," I said. *Great small talk*, I thought to myself. *Real smooth.*

Cheryl just waited.

"Cheryl…I was wondering if you wanted to go to the movies with me this weekend?"

There was a long, long silence on the other line. Then, I heard the dial tone. "Cheryl?" I couldn't believe it. "Cheryl?"

"Earl!" Matt whispered. "What happened?"

"She hung up." I looked at Matt and saw the pity and surprise in his eyes.

"Wow" he said. "That's cold."

Cheryl and I mostly avoided each other for the rest of the year. She never told me why she hung up on me, but in my mind, she didn't have to. It was because I was Black. It was always because I was Black.

I didn't let it show, but that rejection left a very deep bruise. I had put myself out there, and my worst fears had been confirmed. There were places I was just better off not going. I was lucky to have some good friends like Matt, Riles, Speed, John, and JR. We spent long weekend nights in each other's basements, killing orcs in our Dungeons and Dragons campaigns or playing Intellivision instead of going out to meet girls. We were safe down there, at least, and that was enough for a while.

Mr. Toll and Thomas Jefferson

I was hiding underground with my friends on weekends, and I was still laying low at school. Until one day, in Mr. Toll's seventh-grade American history class. We were covering the Founding Fathers, and that week was all about Thomas Jefferson.

Mr. Toll went on and on about Jefferson's unique genius—his writing skill, his vision of a democratic, independent society. I felt a familiar buzzing anger, but I could have pushed it down and let him finish.

But that day, the anger was moving through me, faster and hotter than usual.

Mr. Toll droned on, explaining how Jefferson was a great American hero, an inventor, a true Renaissance man, blah blah blah. My throat tightened and my stomach hardened into a knot. All my old reflexes were telling me just to bury what I had to say. But I just couldn't do it.

My hand went up. Mr. Toll looked surprised.

"We're calling Thomas Jefferson one of the greatest men in history," I started, almost in a whisper. "But he owned slaves."

All of my classmates turned in their seats. Mr. Toll's face puckered, like he had smelled something unpleasant.

"I'm not sure that I understand your point, Earl," he said.

"My point," I said, hoping he didn't see my shaking hands, "is that he owned people. He believed that Black people were three-fifths of a human being. He had people whipped."

The class was quiet. I felt the weight of everyone's stares, but I didn't want to stop now.

"He had one of the biggest slave plantations in the South," I said. "He thought my grandparents were worth as much as a horse or a cow. How could he possibly be a hero?"

The bell rang. Mr. Toll's shoulders drooped with relief.

"We'll talk more about this next time," he said, dismissing us all with a wave of his hand. I stuffed my books into my bag and hurried to the door.

"Being a hero doesn't mean that you're perfect," Mr. Toll mumbled as I walked by his desk. I just nodded my head and got out of there.

I was still shaking a little. I knew that there would be no talking more about this next time. But I had found a little bit of my voice, even if some didn't want to hear it.

52 and 32

Even as I fought the undertow of self-doubt, I knew I liked to win. That's another thing I got from my family; the Phalens are competitive people. The family Thanksgiving football games are the stuff of legends. I had a yearslong Ping-Pong rivalry with my brother Steve, and the day I finally beat him, he got so mad he punched the floor and broke his knuckles. I wouldn't say we turn everything into a competition. But once we're in the game, we don't give up.

For a long time, I didn't really compete at school. I knew I was smart, my friends knew I was smart, and I used some of my intelligence to game the system, putting in the minimum of effort for good enough results.

In our sophomore year, each of us had to report to the guidance counselor to get our class ranking. We were told that this number was extremely important—the closer we were to the top, the closer we were to success and glory, in the form of an acceptance to a "good" college. I wasn't sure I cared all that much, but I showed up to my appointment and got my number: Fifty-second out of a class of 400. Not bad, I thought. Practically top 25 percent.

I met up with my friends later and stayed quiet as they swapped their numbers. Most of them were in the top ten—Cristal and Irene were even tied for number one. I was happy for them, but I pushed away a little pang of jealousy.

I love my friends, but let's face it, they're nerds, I told myself.

I shrugged the whole thing off and was walking to my last class when I ran into Janine Greco. I had always liked Janine. She was a perfect cheerleader, always sweet, with a bouncing ponytail. Today, she was in an even perkier mood than usual

"Earl!" She said excitedly. "Can you believe it? I'm number thirty-two in the class!"

That stopped me in my tracks. I smiled, and I'm sure I said congratulations, but I only had one thought.

Janine Greco, twenty spots ahead of me? Over my dead body.

Janine was great, but we'd grown up together, and there was no doubt in my mind that I was the more talented student. She jogged back down the hallway and I made a silent promise to myself.

No more messing around.

From then on, I ditched the Saturday morning cartoons and woke up early to study. I stopped cutting corners on my assignments, even when I knew I could get away with it. I put extra time into studying for exams and stopped letting little distractions get in my way. By the time we graduated, I had climbed into twelfth place. Not bad, although a little part of me still wishes it could have been better.

Sorry, Janine. But thanks for the inspiration.

Leaving Home

In high school, I started going to house parties with my friends, traveling out to the neighboring towns to drink and meet girls. It was fun, it was something to do, but there was a pattern. We'd go to a party, some guy who thought he was tough would throw around a few racial slurs, and my friends Gary and Speed would take him outside and fight. I loved my friends for sticking up for me, but I got tired of the same exhausting cycle. It was time for something different.

My sister Joanie had moved to DC, and I visited her the summer after my freshman year. The two of us were walking across the National Mall with my niece Leah and two neighbors, Chris and Jason, when we passed several cute Black girls my age. They looked quickly at us and then huddled together, whispering and laughing. I was used to getting stared at when I was out with my siblings. I had all but tuned them out just as Joanie smiled and poked me in the ribs

"Earl," she said, "those girls were checking you out."

Oh, I thought. Maybe DC was a good place to be. Maybe I was attractive after all.

I decided I would apply to Georgetown University, in DC. I had a list of other schools my parents wanted me to apply to, but I felt stuck in the college application process. I didn't really know where to begin, and my guidance counselor seemed detached when I came to him for help, like he was just going through the motions. Luckily, I had Mr. Powell.

Mr. Powell had been my teacher in eighth grade before moving to teach at the high school. On the surface, he had been just another teacher—a middle-aged guy with a bit of a potbelly and a crew cut, in a button-down shirt and slacks. He could be long-winded sometimes, and he loved giving us lectures on work ethic and the power of discipline. But underneath his seeming ordinariness, he was special. One of the most special men I have ever met. He valued all of his students like the individuals we were. He asked for our respect, but he took care to respect us as well. I could feel that he valued and respected me. I didn't even have him for English in high school, but I found myself hanging around his classroom after hours. He was just *that* teacher.

One day, he was giving me his theory on the correct training program for improving my basketball handling skills when he stopped himself and looked at me.

"Earl," he asked, "where are you applying for college?"

"Georgetown, Boston College, Villanova, Harvard, and Brown," I told him, "And Williams, because two of my brothers went there and my mom wants me to."

"That's not enough!" Mr. Powell said, in a voice that surprised me. I laughed, taken aback.

"I'm serious, Earl," he said. "Don't let these knuckle-head 'guidance' counselors or teachers steer you wrong. You should be applying to every school in the Ivy League. You're a brilliant student."

I was a little stunned, and I wasn't sure I believed him, but I listened.

Mr. Powell sighed and pushed up his glasses.

"Take out your notebook," he said, "and let's put together a list."

Mr. Powell became my unofficial guidance counselor. He told me he believed in me enough times that it started to sink in. Together we decided on twelve schools: Harvard, Yale, Dartmouth, Brown, Williams, University of Pennsylvania, University of Virginia, Georgetown, Villanova, Boston College, Holy Cross, and Amherst.

That spring, my friends and I started coming home to the fateful acceptance letters. Boston College said yes. So did the University of Pennsylvania. Brown, Williams, Villanova: yes, yes, yes.

And one day, I came home and that fat Georgetown acceptance letter was lying on the kitchen table. I was so excited to see my friends the next day and tell them the news.

I remember my buddy Speed was almost as happy as I was. "You did it, man!" he yelled, clapping me on the back.

I got a wave of congratulations from everybody else. I knew some of them had to have been jealous, but they were nice enough to smile, cheer, give me a hug. Except for Michael Peet. He fixed me with his usual sullen stare.

"It seems like," Michael drawled, "they only want you...because you're Black."

Just like that, I felt the water rising up around me again. I acted like I hadn't even heard him. I watched my friends give each other panicked looks and change the subject.

I was a three-sport captain, a top student, a leader. But I still couldn't win. When they didn't want me, it was because I was Black. Now that I'd been accepted, it was still just because I was Black.

I was the only Norwood student accepted at Georgetown that year. My close friend Di, our class's salutatorian and one of my favorite people, got rejected. Apparently, that didn't sit right with some of the adults whose job it had been to educate both of us for the past four years. A small group of teachers met together and decided they would write to Georgetown themselves. They would try to convince the school to accept Di—and to reject me.

I don't know what happened with my teachers' plan. I do know that no student should ever be made to feel that his teachers are rooting against him. I should never have had to fight just to stay afloat, just to have my right to learn recognized. Not when I could have been using that energy for better things. Children need their cheerleaders, their protectors, their nurturers. We all lose something when they have to go it alone.

My offer at Georgetown wasn't revoked. But when I got into Yale as well, I knew I couldn't pass up the opportunity. It was the best school on my list, and Mr. Powell was right: I needed to aim for the top. I said a reluctant goodbye to the future I'd imagined in DC. I started getting ready for a new world.

CHAPTER 3

An Education

New Man on Campus

Yale is beautiful in the fall, a brochure brought to life. The tall, dignified stone buildings, like monuments to knowledge. The vast libraries. The lush, tree-lined campus greens with beautiful young people walking through them. And I had never met so many Black people my age. Ivy League schools tend to enroll about 8 percent Black students, year after year, and Yale was no different when I was there. Still, that was a lot more Black people than I was used to. I wasn't one of three Black kids in my school anymore. I felt a little bit of culture shock—at first, I didn't want to go to the Black parties because I was afraid that everyone would find out

I couldn't dance. In the end, there were too many cute women there for me to stay away forever. But I felt like I had some catching up to do.

When I met Wilmot Augustus Allen II—Motty—I knew that I was grateful to be at Yale. Our dorm rooms were right next to each other, and soon we were like brothers. We didn't look that much alike, but we spent so much time together that people mixed up our names. I didn't even mind it that much. Motty was confident and funny, the kind of guy everyone liked to be around. And he really knew how to dress. Motty dreamed big and didn't apologize for it. Today, he runs his own business connecting entrepreneurs across the African diaspora.

Back then, we used to go and shoot hoops in our basement gym, early in the morning. One morning, we were walking back to the dorms, talking about an editorial that had been published in the school paper. One of the columnists had written an anti-affirmative action letter, claiming that considering race in admissions meant there was no way to tell if students were "truly qualified."

"Maybe he has a point," I said. "You know that there's no way to tell if Black people get an unfair advantage in admissions."

Motty stopped and just stared at me. "Earl," he panted, hands on his knees. "That's the dumbest thing I've ever heard you say."

I stopped and stared back. And we both just started laughing. He was right, of course. It really was dumb. Yale, like other schools of its kind, had far more legacy students—students whose applications had been boosted by their parents' donations—than students admitted due to affirmative action. Here I was, succeeding at one of the best schools in the country and still letting some College Republicans influence my thinking. I wasn't in Norwood anymore.

Student to Scholar

At first, I fell back on old habits at Yale. I was the student in the back, trying not to say anything that would get me noticed. But in Professor Weaver's class, something changed.

Professor Weaver was a trim, professionally dressed white woman in her forties. She was poised and cordial, if a little steely. The class was Sociology 101: an intro to the history and theory of people in groups. The readings were from thousands of years of human history, everything from Plato to Martin Luther King Jr.

Professor Weaver was a careful reader. She spoke about each text like she had committed it to memory. Her conservative bent was subtle, but evident. She had little patience for the idea that race still played an important role in American society. One day in class, she gave an admiring lecture on the ideas of William Julius Wilson. Wilson was a Black sociology professor whose academic star rose during the Reagan era. In the late 1970s, he published a book called *The Declining Significance of Race*. He argued that Black people were not really held back by racial discrimination, the way they had been in the past. Instead, African Americans, like people from other groups, suffered mostly from things like poverty and rising unemployment.

"In today's America, race alone is not a limiting influence on a person's potential success," Professor Weaver explained.

I couldn't believe what I was hearing. White women didn't clutch their purses when I passed by them on the street because they thought I was poor. I didn't have slurs screamed at me from cars because people thought my jeans looked secondhand. I found myself raising my hand.

"Actually," I said, "Black people of all social classes still face discrimination all the time."

Unlike Mr. Toll, Professor Weaver didn't back down from a challenge. She turned her head slowly, like an owl, and trained her calm stare on me.

"That's an interesting opinion," she said. "What's your evidence to support it?"

Professor Weaver had a strict philosophy of classroom participation. Anyone who wanted to comment on a reading had to be able to explain what the author was saying. If you could do that, then your opinions were welcomed—encouraged, even.

The only way I could participate was to be prepared. I felt my competitive drive kick in. I could play Professor Weaver's game and win.

I read all of the class materials in advance. The first reading was just a general skim, to get the main idea of each text. On the second reading, I would pick out the most prominent arguments and evaluate their strengths and weaknesses. Was the author truly supporting what they had to say? Were they making assumptions I could challenge? Where were the weak links in their logic?

Before class, I would review what I read and make sure my outline was clear. Over lunch, I turned my friends into my roundtable, seeing if they could help me understand a theory better. If their arguments were better than mine, I debated them until I strengthened my own point of view.

Each week, I prepared more, and each week, I spoke more. Each week, Professor Weaver heard me out, even when she grimaced at what I had to say. My old nervousness never went away completely, but I knew what I was talking about, and it showed.

I got an A- in that class. I thought I deserved an A, but I knew that for all her scholarly rigor, Professor Weaver was swayed by her own not-so-empirical feelings. I didn't care. In a way, I was grateful. I got something better than an A. Professor Weaver taught me to pay close attention to other people's arguments, even when I thought they were wrong. Especially when I thought they were wrong.

Cristal

I started speaking up inside the classroom, and my confidence outside it grew as well. Back in high school, I had had a crush on Cristal for three years. She was beautiful and incredibly smart, and I loved her ambition. When I was sixteen, I didn't even try to make anything happen between us. She was the valedictorian, and she headed to Harvard after graduation. Our freshman fall, we saw each other again, at the Harvard-Yale game, and finally kissed for the first time. I fell hard, and so did she. We talked for hours on the phone, traveled to see each other most weekends. I'd wanted to be with her for so long, and now she saw the new me, a better me.

One night in December, Cristal called me late at night. When I answered the phone, I could tell she'd been crying.

"They kicked me out," she said in a small voice, trying to calm her sobs.

"They" were Cristal's parents. Cristal had always been close to her mom and dad, and they adored their accomplished valedictorian daughter. But now, her parents were threatening to stop paying for college.

Cristal's parents were from the Middle East, but as far as they were concerned, they were white. They claimed that Cristal was putting herself at risk by dating interracially. I knew they weren't threatening to disown their daughter because she had a boyfriend of a different ethnicity. It was because I was Black.

Cristal told me that if our relationship was going to last, she wanted me to go talk to her family. I'd heard that her brother had been telling people back in Norwood that if he saw me, he'd break my legs and throw me in a ditch. But I loved Cristal, and I didn't want to lose her. So that Christmas break, I paid a visit to her parents' house.

"Earl," her mother greeted me at the door, with a warm smile that was just a bit too wide. "Come in."

Her father welcomed me inside, offered me a water, asked how school was going.

I didn't feel like small talk.

"School's fine," I said, "but I know that you think it's wrong for me to date your daughter."

"No, no," her dad said gently, still trying to look friendly, "you're a nice young man."

He brought out a series of excuses. There are evil people in the world, people who won't accept this. They'll make our daughter's life harder. We wouldn't want to put you, her, or your family in danger. What about the children?

I cut to the chase. I knew Cristal's dad was a man of faith.

"Do you think we are all God's children?" I asked him.

"Yes," he said.

"Do you believe that God loves you more than he loves me because you are white and I am Black?"

"No," he said, with that same uncertain smile, "God loves all of his children equally."

"Then why are you saying that just because there are evil people in the world, Cristal and I shouldn't date?" I asked, my voice firm and clear despite the trembling inside.

It was the moment of truth. Either he was going to tell me that despite God's will, he wasn't going to have his daughter date a Black man, or he was stuck. In the end, he just repeated himself, more quietly and more politely, until I got up and shook his hand, and he showed me to the door.

I had done it. I'd found the courage I hoped was there, the voice that was getting stronger. Cristal's parents backed down, and she and I kept seeing each other.

Organizational Behavior

Good education helps you discover the world. Great education helps you discover yourself. Professor Herbert showed me that.

Professor Herbert was young and energetic, a stocky Black man with warm eyes and a big, thick beard. His class had the vague, boring-sounding name of Organizational Behavior. I wasn't sure what to expect, but I had heard some good things. It wasn't long before the professor's experimental side came out. I walked into class in the second week to find the professor absent and all the tables and chairs rearranged. There were instructions on the blackboard for us to sort ourselves into two groups: first names A-L on the left, and first names M-Z on the right. We did as we were told, and when he walked in five minutes later, there were two gossiping clusters on either side of the room. Professor Herbert's TA helped him draw a line in the middle of the room dividing one group from the other. We were under strict instructions not to cross it.

Professor Herbert and the TA left the room again. When they came back, the TA was carrying a big pile of cushions that he helped the M-Zs place on our chairs. The TA joked around with them, saying that they deserved to be comfortable after so many hours sitting in Yale's awful lecture halls. He didn't speak to us at all. When Professor Herbert came back, he had a bag full of grapes, crackers, and cheese—for the M-Zs. All the food stayed strictly on the right side of the line, professor's orders.

At this point, all of us in class understood what was going on. The difference in treatment between A-Ls and M-Zs was obvious. But the thing I'll never forget is how quickly we all adapted to it anyway. It didn't matter that only five minutes before, none of us would have dreamed of dividing ourselves up by first name. This was the way the class worked now.

Everyone adjusted a little differently. Some of my classmates walked, laughing, right up to the line, to try to sneak some extra food to their A-L friends. This made the militant M-Zs angry, and they tried to rat out the food-givers for reaching their hands across the tape. Some of the A-Ls started to get upset, complaining and asking to switch groups. Others just sat on the floor, meek and checked out, waiting quietly for class to be over. Some M-Zs started bonding with people they'd never talked to before about their first-class status. I was too riveted by what I was seeing to do more than sit and watch. It was like a stage play of my childhood, condensed into ten minutes. I had never realized just how quickly, and how completely, people will internalize the way society treats them.

Of course, that was Professor Herbert's point. He didn't want us to get good at following his classroom rules. He wanted us to interrogate our own beliefs and behaviors. His writing assignments read like journal prompts, asking us to dissect the values of our families, schools, hometowns. I saved many of my assignments from Professor Herbert's class. I wrote about the kind of role models I had and hadn't seen growing up. I wrote about what I thought made me good enough in other people's eyes—why I wanted to date certain women, why it took me so long to feel OK speaking in class, why I spent hours in the gym training for basketball but hated it when people assumed I was a basketball player. Professor Herbert opened up a new dimension of learning, beyond arguments and evidence. He helped me see and decode the unspoken lessons life teaches us. I don't really remember anything from the

Organizational Behavior textbook, but I'll never forget the way that class made me feel.

Team Captain

In high school, I had been a three-sport athlete—golf, basketball, and track. At Yale, I dedicated myself to basketball and gained twenty pounds of muscle, but team politics and some disappointments meant I only made it one season past JV. So when I joined the Jonathan Edwards residential college intramural football team, I was mostly looking to flirt, hang out, and blow off some steam. My freshman year, I became the team's top scorer— my nickname was "god." By my sophomore year I was team captain. I decided this would be my path to glory, no matter how small. We were going to win the intramural championship.

It was a reach. Jonathan Edwards had only gone 1-11 my freshman year. The team was better my sophomore year, but not that much better: 6-6. To win it all, we needed everyone to believe. The good news was that we hadn't lost any of our games by a large point margin. I got everyone to commit to two weeks of practice, and we started sketching out our plays. In the end, it worked. We won twelve straight games and intramural fame.

For me, the victory was personal. I never choked on the field, and I came through for my friends when it counted. It was one of the few times that I can remember setting a goal, following through, and achieving it completely. In high school, a nagging fear had told me I didn't deserve to be a leader, to get the win and the credit. I was starting to tell that fear it was wrong.

The next year, we had an intramural championship to defend. That was when some more lessons came in. I was just as committed to victory as I had been before, and I took it all very seriously—more or less. I used to sign off my motivational letters this way:

"Every morning when you wake up, and every night before you go to bed, face towards New Haven, place your right hand on your chest, and hum the JE fight song."

The problem was, pulling off an underdog win and defending a new championship were completely different leadership challenges. We had decided the only way to go was up, and that we needed not just to win but to shut out every other team. Instead of being excited to grow together, we were obsessed with not losing any ground. After a narrow victory, rather than shrug our shoulders and head to the mess hall, we would try to squeeze in an extra practice.

We actually won the championship again, but a lot of the joy got sucked out of the experience. That was a powerful lesson, too, one I use in my work today: Don't become a victim of your own expectations. Teamwork is about looking to the future, not about competing with the past. And when it comes to communication with people outside your organization, whether it's your intramural rival or a possible investor: under promise and over deliver. And always have your teammates' backs.

My senior year, my friends and I widened our vision. We set up something called Project Shelter, convincing local businesses to sponsor the Yale touch football program and donate money on the championship team's behalf. We only raised $2,300 of our $10,000 goal, but it was something. When the time came to deliver the check, though, I couldn't go to the shelter myself. I think I was afraid it would be awkward. I didn't want to have to mingle with the folks at the shelter, make small talk. I was proud of what I'd led our team to do, but my fear still nagged at me, too. What was holding me back?

Graduation

After Yale, I was headed to Harvard Law. But I had no idea what career law school was going to prepare me for. My parents had insisted that I have a summer job all through college, and I had spent time working at the Bank of Boston. My job was to sort through incoming credit card bills. I had to match the account number on each customer's check with the number in the bank's records. It was exactly as boring as it sounds. My parents had wanted the job to teach me something, and it certainly had. It taught me why so many people hate going to work every morning, and it taught me that a lot of managers have absolutely no idea what they're doing. Most importantly, it taught me that I needed work I could feel passionate about. I wanted to lose my fear of community service. My friends and family still saw me as the kid who still had his mom and best friend Tuck call to wake him up for exams. I knew I could push myself further than that.

Graduation was bittersweet. I hated saying goodbye to all my friends, even if I couldn't understand why they were headed off to Wall Street or consulting firms. After some serious reflection, I had deferred Harvard Law for a year and, with the encouragement of my closest friend, Anne, signed up with the Lutheran Volunteer Corps. The Corps housed small groups of young graduates, giving us a living stipend, and assigning us to service opportunities across the country.

I ended up in my favorite city, Washington, DC. Within days, I was the new assistant coordinator at Luther Place Shelter, an organization that provided a living space for homeless women looking to transition to full-time housing. My year there was the most important one of my life.

CHAPTER 4

Finding My Purpose

A Life of Service

In DC, I shared a home with several other volunteers from the Corps. The other people at the house didn't seem to be my kind of people, at least not at first. They were kind and dedicated, but we rarely talked about sports or pop culture, and it sometimes felt that we had almost nothing in common. I remember being shocked that they'd never heard "The Humpty Dance" by Shock G—it was everywhere on the radio back in 1990. I played it for my roommate Karland and he sat motionless, frowning with concentration at every word.

Karland almost jumped out of his chair in response to the lyrics referring to a female being fat and ticklish.

"Earl!" he said. "Did he just say what I think he did?"

"Well, yeah," I admitted, "but he's just being funny."

"I don't think it's funny," Karland said, with a sincerity that took the bite out of his words, "to put down another human being."

I didn't know what to say to that—and I couldn't fault Karland for his feelings—so I turned Shock G off. And he stayed off for the rest of the year. There was no television either: my roommates felt that TV was a way of avoiding true human connection. I missed the Super Bowl for the first time, and March Madness, and all my favorite shows. We ate simple, mostly vegetarian meals, and we gathered every two weeks to reflect with each other and discuss social justice. It was a busy life, almost monastic in its rhythms.

At the shelter, I was acutely aware that I didn't know what I was doing. On my first day as assistant coordinator at Luther Place Shelter, I met with a young woman named Robin. She was nineteen to my twenty-one—we could have been at school together. I struggled to seem professional and competent as she sat across the desk and asked me for my help.

Robin was the mother to a young son, and she was five months pregnant with her second child. She had been told that because of a recent arrest for prostitution, she could no longer see her son. She was struggling her hardest not to use, for the sake of her toddler and her unborn child, but she felt the weight of her addiction pressing down on her every day. But the reason she had come to us, she said, was that she didn't know how to deal with devastating news she had just received from the clinic.

"They told me I was positive for HIV," Robin told me, starting to cry. I had to hold back my own tears as I looked frantically around the room.

"Here, let me get you a Kleenex," I said, finally finding a box in a corner.

What else did I have to offer in that moment? I was used to looking down on women like Robin, or, more accurately, not thinking about them at all. I knew it, and I was ashamed of it. I hoped she couldn't feel me stumble over the wrong words, that I didn't sound totally useless when I said I would make sure to set up a meeting for her with our director, Judy. To my surprise, Robin was grateful. We hugged, and she thanked me for taking the time to listen. I was grateful, too. Robin had been generous enough to let me help her. She taught me that every act of service is a cooperation. The people we serve, the scholars we teach, teach us just as much.

A True Community

That cooperation sustained me every day. I had never seen a community like the one the women at the shelter created. They were very different people, brought together by terrible circumstances. About a third of the women were mentally ill and had lived previously at psychiatric institutions in DC, before a facilities shutdown had forced them to move. The other women tended to be younger, struggling with homelessness and often battling addiction and other health issues. Many of the women had suffered domestic abuse, and the mothers among them were separated from their children.

There were the usual personality clashes and petty arguments. But the women of the shelter, who had every reason in the world to be bitter about how life had treated them, were the most generous and supportive people I had ever met. If one woman was feeling sick, the others would notice right away and let her keep her seat while they fixed her a plate. The women at the main shelter slept together in cots on a converted basketball court. They kept their spare, crowded home clean and calm, knowing that many of their roommates had a sense of peace that was fragile and easily disturbed. I watched a group of four women, all of them hurting mothers, comfort a fifth who was overwhelmed with grief at being away from her daughters. They celebrated each time a woman made the move from the shelter to transitional housing. Her triumphs were bound up with their own.

Still, many of the women in the shelter led dangerous lives, and we couldn't always keep the danger at bay. On my second day at Luther Place, a resident's ex-boyfriend came into the common area and slashed her new boyfriend's throat. He almost bled out on the floor. Our director Judy was there, as she always was, and staunched the blood until the paramedics came. He survived, but the incident rattled me.

One of our residents, Alisha, had been suspended for coming to the shelter high and disrupting the other residents. One day, she came back, angry and disoriented, and started stealing other residents' clothes. There was a commotion, and the women asked me to confront her. She wouldn't leave, even after smashing dishes and refusing to hand over the clothes. When I put my hands on her shoulders and tried to march her out the door, she punched me in the jaw. Finally, she left, and someone called the police on her way out. I was fine, if still a little angry. But I heard rumblings that Alisha's boyfriend was coming for revenge.

Later that evening, I was walking between our buildings when I saw a real-life John Henry step out of the shadows. He was six-foot-six at least, pure muscle in overalls and no shirt. He had a strong, confident walk and a blank expression on his face. In his right hand was a machete.

I froze. *Oh snap!*

"Earl?" the man asked, in a deep and gentle voice. "Are you OK?"

I had never seen this man before in my life. How did he know my name?

"I'm all right," I said.

"Some of the girls said you were in trouble, so I was coming to help."

I thanked him, still a little stunned. We were standing closer now, and he loosened his grip on the machete.

"You do a lot of good work for the women here," he said. "I would never let anything happen to you."

I felt completely safe in that moment. I never saw that man again, or even learned his name. But it was so good to know that someone was looking out for me, that I was part of a community that had my back.

Black Pioneers, Black Role Models

My days at the shelter were long. I came in every afternoon, to supervise the volunteers for dinner, and didn't leave until after breakfast the next morning. Work was six days a week, fifteen hours a day. Even with the grueling hours, my mind and spirit felt excited and alive. Whenever I had a spare moment, I read.

I would go to used bookstores and pick up anything I thought might have something to teach me.

At one small place in DC, I found a series of pamphlets—simply but sturdily produced, with a staple in the middle holding the brightly colored pages together. The series was called *Black Pioneers*. There were hundreds of pamphlets, and I read every one I could find. I started to see just how much I hadn't been told.

These were not the three or four well-known Black heroes I had grown up with: there were so many more. These were scientists, entrepreneurs, people of undeniable power and intellect, "ordinary" people who made extraordinary, collective sacrifice. I read about the still-unsolved mysteries of ancient Egyptian architecture, the vast medieval libraries of Timbuktu. I read Phyllis Wheatley and Sojourner Truth. I discovered American innovators like Lewis Latimer, the man who worked alongside Alexander Graham Bell and Thomas Edison, and without whom there would be no lightbulb. Innovators like Garrett Morgan, who created the traffic light. A Black man created the traffic light?

I was struck by the story of Benjamin Banneker, a mathematician and scientist born in Maryland in 1731. Like Benjamin Franklin, Banneker published a yearly almanac, using his knowledge of astronomy to correctly predict solar eclipses. Like Thomas Jefferson, he was a farmer, a writer, and an inventor, but Banneker was also a champion of civil rights. Unlike Benjamin Franklin and Thomas Jefferson, he had never once been mentioned when I was in school. I remembered that seventh-grade conversation with Mr. Toll, how shocked he had been when I pointed out Jefferson's slave owning and his hypocrisy. But Banneker had made the same point about Jefferson—to Jefferson—200 years earlier. In 1791, he wrote a letter to Jefferson, urging him to live up to his own values and take action to end the enslavement and oppression of Black Americans. Jefferson wrote a brief, polite note back, promising to send a copy of Banneker's almanac to France. *We'll talk about this more next time.*

Soon, I was reading five books a week, desperate to correct the gaps in my own education. The *Black Pioneers* led me to Carter G. Woodson, the father of Black History. Woodson was born in 1875, to formerly enslaved parents. He earned a PhD from Harvard and started a career as a historian and professor at Howard. Woodson realized quickly that the history of Black Americans hadn't just been ignored, it had been actively suppressed. Black students who wanted to succeed in the world of education were taught that they had to embrace this anti-Black indoctrination, to disown Black achievement and see white cultural history as superior.

In his landmark book, *The Miseducation of the Negro*, Woodson urged his readers to educate themselves, to read widely and reject the programming of traditional education. He urged Black people to step into their power by thinking for themselves. I was doing exactly that, and I felt my mind sharpen from the effort. But what about all that wasted time? What if Black children never had that burden of unlearning in the first place?

Sometimes, as I read, I would be hit with waves of fresh, overwhelming anger. I hated most white people for perpetuating a Holocaust of twenty million to one hundred million Africans over hundreds of years. For sweeping that history away and daring to promote a myth of progress instead. I wrote to my friends, telling them about everything I had been learning, about Marcus Garvey, the lost dream of Pan-Africanism, the history we hadn't been taught. I wrote to my mom, and to David, telling them about my new feelings of hatred. I know they wrote me back, but I can't remember what those letters said. It was as if I needed them to hear me, but I also knew they couldn't really help me with what I was feeling. I was just beginning to understand my anger—I just needed my family to hear my journey.

I turned to the work of Malcolm X, who taught me that anger at injustice is a powerful force and a natural reaction. Anger is a motivator, the impetus to fight battles that need to be fought. Malcolm X had been bored in prison, unwilling to let his intellectual gifts waste away. So he started reading, and like me, he felt his anger wake up. He became one of the greatest orators of his time, a man who knew exactly how to cite his opponents' sources. Malcolm X was condemned, in his own time and afterward, for his support of violence against segregationists, racists, anyone who stood in the way of Black self-determination. To those people, he simply quoted the Declaration of Independence. What was the American Revolution, if not a violent struggle for freedom? Malcolm had channeled his anger into change. And his initial hatred of white people fell away, over time. Hatred was a distraction, and he came to realize allies in the fight against oppression came from all races and all classes. He embraced all people who were committed to his mission. Maybe I could do the same.

After immersing myself in Malcolm X's work, I read all of Dr. Martin Luther King Jr.'s speeches, as well as his essays and letters. Of course, I had known about him my whole life: Martin Luther King Jr. was my mother's hero and my namesake. In school, we had been taught to contrast Malcolm X and Dr. King, to see the nobility of non-violent protest as a rebuke to Malcolm X's demand for justice by any means necessary.

When I read through Dr. King's work again, I saw something very different. I saw a man who didn't shy away from conflict, who was unflinching in his criticisms of American society. Dr. King wasn't asking to be accepted by the America he knew; he was looking to lead it into something better. Anyone who was willing to join the cause was welcome, but there was no compromise when it came to the dignity of Black lives and the urgency of the struggle.

I felt that same sense of urgency. I knew, after a year at Luther Place, that I was called to a life in service. There was so much work to do, and no time to waste. I was about to continue my studies at Harvard, but thanks to my year of service and reading, I was armed with an education of my own making, a deeper connection to the fight for Black freedom.

New School, New Problems

When I left DC for Cambridge and Harvard Law's campus, I was back in a world I recognized—the arena of grades, competition, rankings. My classmates were studious and polished, but they had TVs and didn't mind listening to Shock G. I made some great friends, but the atmosphere in class could be tense and combative. I was far from the only one there who liked winning. Even the intramural basketball games were cutthroat.

By the end of my 1L year, I was more than a little exhausted. Academically, I had been insecure. Romantically, I had gotten reckless.

I had come a long way from that shy, Dungeons and Dragons–playing middle schooler who thought every girl would hang up on him. After all, in college I had finally started seeing Cristal. After I confronted her father, we stayed together for a few years, but Cristal's rift with her family put a lot of pressure on our relationship. We would argue, too often, and eventually we broke up. I started seeing other people at school, hoping to find something easier and more peaceful.

At Yale, I fell in love with my classmate Kim, a gorgeous Black woman with curly hair and a smattering of freckles across her face. We used to eat at the dining hall and argue over our readings, and I loved listening to her soft, confident voice, with its hint of a lisp, even when she was telling me I had no idea what I was talking about. She graduated a year before I did, left, and broke my heart.

My year at Luther Place, I was in a long-distance relationship with Anne, my best friend from Yale. In undergrad, I had spent years ignoring her crush on me, not wanting to ruin my friendship with someone so purehearted, one of the only people I knew I could trust completely. During our senior year, the friendship became something more, and the year after college, I poured my heart out to her in letters and phone calls. And when we didn't last, I came to Harvard single and a little unmoored.

I looked good, though. I had put on another twenty pounds of muscle in college, and I lifted weights four days a week all through my year at Luther Place. I met beautiful women pretty much the moment I stepped on Harvard's campus. I played the field pretty hard, and I left some hurt feelings in my wake. I was Mr. August in the 1991 Black Men of Harvard Law School calendar, posing in a skin-tight black wetsuit on a surfboard I had never used. Some of the women of the Black Law Students Association objected to me being included on the calendar. They said the last thing I needed was a new way to advertise myself to the student body. But even more women insisted that I needed my own month. At least the calendar helped raise some money for charity. It was one of the few charitable things I had found time to do.

I felt unsettled, conflicted. Harvard was full of opportunities, but I sensed I was losing sight of something important. I decided I would get out of Boston for a while. For my summer internship, I picked an international law program in Jamaica, thinking it would be the change I needed. I would be working on police brutality and habeas corpus at the Jamaican Council for Human Rights.

1 + 1

In Kingston, Jamaica, I had a solid routine—sit-ups in the morning, daily journaling, long talks with my good friend Mylan on my lunch break. My work at the Council kept me busy enough, and I loved meeting the other people on the team. But I missed spending time with kids. I've been an uncle since I was a teenager, and by the time I got to law school, I had twenty-three nieces and nephews. I wanted to see if there was a way I could help children. I approached my boss at the Council, Florezelle, and she agreed that I could have one afternoon off a week to volunteer at a nearby orphanage. She arranged it all with a friend of hers who worked there, and I reported for duty that week.

Maxfield Park Orphanage was made up of ten houses. About fifteen to twenty-five kids, ages six to eighteen, lived in each house. They were supervised by a housemother, who served as teacher, guardian, and supervisor all in one. My job was to be her assistant during afternoon lessons. I showed up on my first day, ready to meet the housemother, and was called to talk with the flustered-looking director instead.

"Earl," she said, "I have some good news and some bad news."

The bad news was that the housemother had quit that morning. The good news, according to her, was that I would get to be head teacher for a group of twenty-one children I had never met, starting right that moment.

No walk into a classroom has ever been as scary to me as the one I took that day. Even the most dreaded law school exams were no comparison. I tried to come up with a lesson I could teach off the top of my head to twenty-one children, ages six to eighteen, and drew a furious blank. I took a breath, walked into the class, and saw forty-two expectant eyes staring back at me.

"Good morning, class," I said. "My name is Earl."

A twelve-year-old boy's hand shot up.

"Yes?"

"We're not allowed to call teachers by their first names," he said. "It's not respectful."

"Oh," I said. "Then you can call me Mr. Earl." *Lesson number one.*

"I'm Mr. Earl, and I'll be your teacher for a while." All forty-two eyes stayed on me.

"I'm from the United States," I continued, "I go to school in Boston, Massachusetts, and am working down here this summer. I was put up for adoption when I was a baby and lived in two foster homes…" What was I saying? I thought they might feel uplifted by my story, but I heard myself starting to ramble. The eyes were still staring, not at all unkindly.

I realized that that was about as far as I could make it on my own. If we were going to work together, I would need to count on my students' help.

"So," I said, "what do you normally work on?"

The twelve-year-old's hand was back in the air.

"We usually have math time, reading time, and then free time to color and draw and play educational games," he explained proudly.

"That sounds great," I said. "Let's get to work."

I was circulating around the classroom when a little girl with braids and a loose tooth called me over for help.

"Mr. Earl," she asked, "what's one plus one?"

"Well," I said, "one plus one is two." *So far so good.*

"Why?" the girl asked, looking up at me.

That was a question law school hadn't prepared me for. Why was one plus one two?

"I think, it's just good to remember that if you have one, and then another one, and then they combine together…" I was stalling for time when a girl of about sixteen came over with some crayons in her hand. She laid one on the table.

"Here," she explained gently, "you take one crayon. Then"—she laid another—"you take one more crayon and then you count them. Now, how many crayons are there?"

"Two?" the little scholar answered.

"That's right!" she said.

The girl's eyes lit up. *She knew how to add.*

She turned to me. "Give me another problem!"

"Okay," I said, "what is two plus one?"

"You take two crayons," she explained out loud, "and add them to one crayon, and then count them. One, two, three. Three," she said, beaming with confidence.

"That's correct…wow, you are smart!" I said encouragingly. "So smart."

She beamed. She was smart, and she knew it. I had been there to help, but she had learned it herself.

This was it.

I had known I wanted to serve. Now I finally knew how. I would help children learn, and I would be there to watch them start believing in themselves.

The moment my teaching day ended, I ran to the nearest pay phone and called my parents collect in Norwood.

"Mom! Dad!" I said, almost out of breath. "I'm dropping out of law school!"

I told them everything—the promotion to head teacher, the crayons, watching a young girl feel pride in her own intelligence.

"I need to stop wasting time and become a teacher," I said.

There was a loaded silence on the phone. My mom spoke first.

"That's wonderful, Earl. We're so happy for you."

My dad couldn't help himself.

"But you should stay in school, Earl."

I tried to explain to them that law school didn't matter anymore. I had found something I really loved doing, after years of searching and doubt. I could make a real difference, here with these kids.

My dad's voice was calm, patient. He didn't raise his voice or try to scare me. Like an expert banker, he presented me with the risks and rewards.

I would have to train from scratch as a teacher, but I only had two years left in my law training.

I could use a law degree to advocate for children, even go into educational policy.

A degree from Harvard Law would open doors for me for the rest of my life.

I couldn't know what I might want to do in the future—why not keep all my options open? I didn't want to abandon a law career only to regret it later.

I put on a good debate over the phone, but in the end, I agreed to stay in school. My dad was right: Harvard Law would open doors. But I went back to my 2L year with a mission in mind. What my parents didn't realize was that I wasn't really persuaded. I knew, that moment in Jamaica, that I would find my way into education. That was the day my dream was born.

My first Christmas as a Phalen

Singing at my sister's wedding

Me and my dad

5 Handicap in Golf as a High School Senior

High School game against rival

At my Senior Prom

My mom and sister Mary at my college graduation

High School Graduation

Yale College Basketball

Summer internship with Senator Ted Kennedy

1997 President's Service Award

Enjoying parent's 60th Anniversary

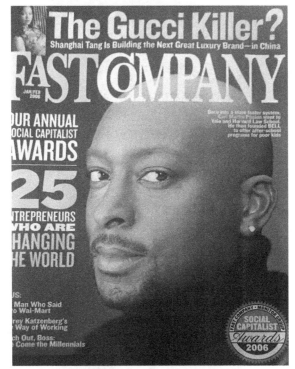

Featured in Fast Company

My birth mother, Maryann

My birth father, grandmother and uncles and aunts

One of my godchildren and one of my 54 nephews and nieces

My brother, Nate

Me, Angie, Red Sox President, Larry Lucchino and my mentor, Professor Charles Ogletree

Featured in Essence Magazine

First Lady Michelle Obama and Dr. Jill Biden

BET National Award for Community Service

Coaching Boys Varsity Team

James Rosemary Phalen Leadership Academy becomes first A-rated Middle High School on the Far Eastside of Indianapolis

Joyful time at Thanksgiving with the family

CHAPTER 5

The Mission Takes Shape

All A's

In the fall of 1991, I went back to Harvard more committed to my studies than ever. I hadn't forgotten my promise to myself, or my call to my parents from that telephone booth in Jamaica. But I couldn't get a moment from first year out of my head. I had retreated to one of the lecture hall men's rooms, after a Torts final I felt lucky to survive. I was washing my hands and praying for a B when I overheard two white guys talking at the urinals.

"I aced that exam," one of them said. "I'm pretty sure I got an A."

"An A?" The other guy laughed. "Trust me, I got an A plus."

They zipped up, washed their hands, and walked out, still joking with an easy arrogance.

I was stunned. At a Black Law Students Orientation, they had told all of us that law school was a struggle for everyone, that we should expect to get mostly Bs. Here these two guys were, talking like A pluses were just ripe for the taking.

If they can do it, I thought, *then so can I.*

Ever since my conversation with Janine Greco back in high school, I had known that I had another gear, and that true academic achievement was possible for me. Still, I had never gotten all A's before. There was always some subject I let slide, some challenge I decided wasn't worth the extra effort. I had always fallen short of a perfect record, and I had also spent my whole life haunted by a sense of unmet potential. Now, I was at Harvard Law, the apex of academic achievement. If I was ever going to prove I could make it to the top, now was the time.

My friend Karla was the most put-together student I knew. The next time I saw her in the library, I asked her what I needed to do to get all A's.

"Simple," she said, counting off the steps on her fingers. "Take classes you like. Do all the readings on the weekend and build your outlines as you go. Find 2Ls and 3Ls and ask them for their outlines and notes. Make sure you get the old exam questions, too. They're a clue to where the professor is going. Get them early and review them throughout the semester."

It was simple. But it wasn't easy. I knocked myself out that first 2L semester, and months of late nights and marathon study sessions paid off. I knew before the grades even came in that I had done it. The As on the transcript were just for the record.

I think I put something to rest that semester. There was no wasted potential, no summit I had to gaze up at, wondering why I wasn't there. All that outlining and exam reviewing was worth it just for that feeling. After that semester, though, I didn't see the point in striving for a 4.0. I knew my real passion was outside the law school classroom. For the rest of my Harvard career, I was content to get A's and B's. I had other work to do.

What Are We Going to Do?

Since returning from Jamaica, I had been eager to get back into teaching. I had a group of friends who shared my interest in community service, and we looked together for mentoring opportunities. We began at the Boys and Girls Club in Roxbury, Massachusetts, where we were invited to lead an after-school mentoring program. We signed on for two visits a week. One day a week, we would help a group of about twenty middle schoolers with their homework and projects. The other day, we would just get a pizza, play basketball, and hang out—give the kids some time to relax and talk about whatever was on their minds.

On the first tutoring day, my girlfriend Drea, Drew, Francis, Joe, Eric, and I got in the car and made the half-hour trip to Roxbury. We were all in a good mood, cracking jokes and talking over each other. It felt good to have something other than case law to look forward to. The Boys and Girls Club had set us up in an empty basketball court, and the six of us spread out on the bleachers, each with our little crew of students. They were a friendly group, happy to recite what grade they were in and what they were studying. And they were obviously bright.

I had a group of three sixth graders, two boys and a girl, who were all in the same math class. They had a packet due the next day on multiplying and dividing fractions. The first problem looked something like:

1/3 x 2

I asked how we could rewrite the problem so that the number two looked like a fraction too, with a numerator and a denominator.

No one knew.

I took a step back and wondered if we could say out loud what the problem was asking us to do. After talking it over, I realized that none of the students could take the next step and multiply the fraction—because they didn't know what a fraction was.

For the rest of the hour, we worked slowly backward through some fundamentals. We used circle graphs to talk through wholes and parts, and we practiced writing down numbers and proportions as fractions. I was touched by my group's patience with me, and with each other—that first session was a slog. They learned quickly, but there was so much ground to cover. The smart, engaged kids sitting across from me were still at about a second-grade level in math.

As I worked, I overheard Drea a few seats over, helping an eighth grader work through some basic multiplication exercises. Our eyes met briefly, but we looked away—we didn't want the students to be able to read our thoughts.

At the end of the afternoon, the six of us filed into the car in total silence. You could hear every little squeak of the leather as we shifted in our seats. I think Drew was the one who spoke first.

"What are we going to do?"

We all started talking at once. None of us had realized just how deep the problem was. The administrators at the Roxbury Boys and Girls Club had been somewhat breezy and casual, never letting on that the students they were serving had been so underserved by the educational system that they were years behind in their studies.

Drew was the one who helped us move past our shock and start brainstorming solutions. He was never one to dwell on blame—instead, he had us look calmly at the facts and focus on solutions. A pizza a week wasn't going to help them master elementary math, let alone get into college. If we were going to really help these kids, we needed more resources, more time, and more people. We needed to build something much bigger than just an after-school program: we needed a coordinated effort and a mission. After that car ride, we came together to create BELL.

My Mentors

Those first days of building BELL, I was so lucky to be able to draw on our community at the law school. At Harvard, I was surrounded by some of the smartest and most ambitious Black people I had ever met. I'll never forget one day in Harkness Commons, one of the big graduate centers where the students would go to pick up mail, have a meal, hang out. I was with a Constitutional Law classmate, eating fries and discussing *Terry v. Ohio*. The case is a landmark Supreme Court decision, typical study material for law students. It was the case that established the legality of police stop and frisk policies, and we were arguing about the weaknesses in the Court's opinion, when Barack (Obama), who just happened to overhear, sat down and reminded us of a minor point in the decision like he'd reviewed the whole case that morning. With a cool agility, he spun out the many implications of the distinction between "probable cause" and the Court's new threshold of "reasonable suspicion" of criminal behavior, citing all his sources from memory. I got the feeling that if the justices themselves had been at that table with us, they might have struggled to keep up. I was lucky to know Michelle (Obama) as well; while we never got to work together, she started her community initiatives in Chicago just as BELL was getting off the ground, and we cheered each other on. Years later, it came as no surprise that there was a Senator Obama we could call on to champion legislation for summer learning programs.

I could tell I wasn't the only Black Harvard Law student with big dreams. We were all ambitious, with our own stories about how we were going to change the world. And most of us would eventually find ourselves in the office of Charles Ogletree, the law professor and unofficial mentor of the Black student community, telling him all about our plans. Professor Ogletree later told me that at first, he was skeptical of my commitment to creating BELL. Over the years, he had counseled a lot of students who talked about starting nonprofits or devoting themselves to civil rights, only to listen to the siren call of corporate law once graduation rolled around. When I first came to him for advice on how to get a public service enterprise started, he was polite, but brief.

"But then," he told me later, "you kept coming back."

I'm very grateful that I did—and that I had a mentor like Professor Ogletree to come back to. Tree, as the students called him, was a 1978 Harvard Law graduate, not that much older than we were. By the time we met, he had already had an impressive legal career. He'd worked for eight years as a public defender and hosted a TV show called *Ethics in America*. My first year at Harvard, he agreed to represent Anita Hill when she testified against Clarence Thomas in the infamous Senate Confirmation hearings. It was a risky move at the time: Tree had been up for tenure, and Hill was a lightning rod, a target for a political machine eager to diminish her credibility and destroy her reputation. But Tree stuck by her side, and Anita Hill later spoke of him as one of the most generous, principled, and intelligent men she had ever known.

Professor Ogletree taught me the art of disagreeing without being disagreeable—although admittedly, I am still working on that. He had a knack for communicating passion without overwhelming people. He never compromised his principles or held back his opinions. But his sincerity invited people in, and his sense of humor set them at ease. And he gave his time so generously. Every time faculty was invited to a Harvard Black Law Students Association meeting, Professor Ogletree was there. He took office hours for Black students who had his classes, and he kept his door open for those who didn't. He advocated tirelessly on behalf of students, committed to a vision of a law school that served students equally. I wanted to be the kind of advocate that he was. Eventually, I managed to convince Tree that I was in public service for the long haul, and he ended up serving on my board at BELL for thirteen years. The first program BELL ever launched was the Charles Ogletree Scholarship Fund—a $2,500 college scholarship to graduating seniors from low-income families. I was so proud the first time we presented that check. I'm still proud of the twenty-one scholars we were able to celebrate on their way to college.

When the group of us first started BELL, we decided the acronym stood for Building Enterprises for Learning and Living. Later, it was Building Educated Leaders for Life. From the beginning, though, the name was a tribute to another one of my greatest mentors, Professor Derrick Bell. Professor Bell was the only Black graduate of his law school in 1957, and two years later he gave up a job at the US Justice Department rather than resign his NAACP membership. He parlayed a lost government job into a decades-long career as a civil rights attorney, law professor, and theorist.

Professor Bell had an ability to think beyond the law, to analyze not just the cause-and-effect chain of legal rulings but the diffuse, often surprising ways the law interacts with social and political power. His work on the aftermath of *Brown v. Board of Education*, and the effects of school desegregation on Black communities, resonated deeply with me. Professor Bell pointed out that desegregating schools had removed a systemic injustice, but it had not corrected it. In fact, in the wake of desegregation, the landscape of educational inequality had grown more complex. Black students were sent to schools where they were outnumbered and often unwelcome. Once schools were officially "integrated," Black students who underperformed in school, or couldn't access adequate resources, were blamed when they didn't succeed. And those who did succeed were often "guided" into lower tracks, graded more harshly, and disproportionately disciplined. Professor Bell helped me see that education was inextricably linked with self-determination, equity, self-image, and pride. I knew that a large part of the work ahead for BELL would be convincing our scholars, and our society, that educating Black children still mattered, and that no amount of educational inequality would ever be acceptable. Professor Bell helped show me what the path to justice might look like.

My second year of law school, Professor Bell left Harvard Law for good. He had spoken out against the school's failure to hire a single woman of color on the faculty. He offered the school ten names, respected scholars in their fields; Harvard dragged its heels, and eventually he kept his word and resigned in protest. Before he left, I talked to him about my goals for BELL, my dreams for a nonprofit that provided educational equity as well as other services for the Black community.

"Whatever you do, Earl," he said to me, "do right by the kids." I have always tried to live up to that advice.

Fundraising 101

We came up with an idea for a BELL fundraising gala, to raise money for the scholarship program. Drea loved jazz, so we ran with that and held a Jazz, Rhythm and Blues party. Drew and I figured out how to do the promotions. Felix led logistics and finances, and Joe somehow managed to talk his way into free platters of hors d'oeuvres and several boxes of donated wine. That first Jazz, Rhythm and Blues was one of the best Harvard events I remember. All of Black Harvard showed up and looked good, and the dancing went on until the early morning. The next day, we found out we'd raised $2,100. Not bad at all—and fun enough that we made the Jazz, Rhythm and Blues party our signature gala for years. But a drop in the bucket in terms of running a real nonprofit. I was going to need to know how to raise a lot more money than that if I wanted to get BELL off the ground.

I decided to go straight to the source. I contacted Bayley Mason, the senior development officer at Harvard University, and asked for a meeting.

When I got to Bayley's office, I met a well-heeled but unassuming middle-aged white man. I explained that I was starting my own nonprofit and told him a little bit about BELL's mission. He was warm and easy to talk to, but like Professor Ogletree, he kept it brief. He handed me a little hardbound book called *How to Fundraise*, told me to read it, and sent me on my way.

I read it like a law student—notes, comments, a detailed outline—and asked to meet with Bayley again to discuss my questions.

When we saw each other again in his office, his last bit of reserve had cracked. He smiled at me.

"I didn't expect you to actually read it," he said.

We talked for a while that day, and he gave me some of the basic tools of the fundraising trade. Fundraising is about relationships, he told me. People don't want to just fund a blind proposal. They want a cause they understand and can commit to, and a personal connection to the work they're investing in. Remember that you need three thank-yous in between each request. Don't just thank people when they give you money—reach out, regularly, with your gratitude. And remember that trust is built through networking and introductions.

Fundraising 101 with Bayley Mason was the best course I never took. I was honored when he joined the board of BELL, and I owe all our early fundraising successes to his advice.

Creative Visualization

My friends and I honored our commitment to the Boys and Girls Club and finished out that year at Roxbury. The scholars there were awesome, and we were able to make progress on their math and literacy skills. But we were excited when a group of Black parents from the Agassiz School, a public school in Cambridge, approached us. They had heard about what we were starting to do with BELL, and they wanted our help. Their elementary-school-aged children were already starting to say that they felt disengaged from school, like it "wasn't for them." These parents wanted role models for their kids who would hold them to high standards and encourage them to believe in themselves.

At Roxbury, I never shook the feeling that the administrators were way too cavalier about the educational barriers their scholars were facing. The Agassiz School would be our chance to approach education holistically, bringing Black pride to the forefront of our work with scholars.

At BELL, we started a practice that I use to this day. We call all of our students "scholars," because that's what they are. Learning is a difficult journey, one they approach with bravery and intelligence, day after day. We honor our scholars' effort with the respect, and the high expectations, they deserve. It's common to address learners as scholars now, but it wasn't back when BELL started. We set the tone early, and we stuck to it.

After a few months at the Agassiz School, we'd started to see a lot of scholars come out of their shells, taking pride in their gifts and their progress. But when I came in on report card day, there was still anxiety in the air. One of my scholars, Guy, seemed especially down. He was kicking the leg of his desk with an angry, nervous rhythm.

It was hard not to love Guy. He was a tall, slender kid, with a close fade and a big smile that could light up a room. I worried about him, though. His mom raised him and his older brother alone. Guy idolized his brother, who had recently started making bad choices and running pretty hard in the streets. Even at ten years old, Guy was coming to a crossroads in his life. He was a natural leader, but I could see him starting to lead down the wrong path.

"Hey Guy," I said, "let me see your report card."

"Nah," he said, not meeting my eyes.

"Come on, Guy, take it out of your bag," I insisted.

"Fine!" He stuffed a crumpled paper in my hand. "I just don't want my mom to see it."

I uncrumpled the card and read the bad news: C, C-, D, D, F.

"Not too good, Guy," I said.

"No kidding, man," he snapped back.

"Guy." I crouched down to his level. "You are way too smart for these grades. What happened?"

He started mumbling about his teacher, but I cut him off before he could list his litany of excuses. I knew what was really bothering him. If his grades got too low, his mom might pull him out of football, his main joy. I didn't want that to happen any more than he did.

"You can't change the past," I told him. "But you can control your future. Let's set some goals. What grades do you want to get next semester?"

"C's," he mumbled.

"That's your *goal*?" I responded. "Dream big, Guy. Set high expectations for yourself."

"Okay," he said, "then I want to be on the honor roll."

"That's a great goal," I said. "Now, I want you to close your eyes and picture it."

During my year at Luther Place, I had read a couple self-help books on goals and self-esteem. All of them stressed the importance of creative visualization: picturing what you want and empowering yourself to take the steps to get it. *If you can see it*, the books proclaimed, *you can achieve it*. I sat down with Guy and led him through a series of visualization exercises.

What would it be like to see a report card full of A's and B's? How would you feel, taking a report card like that home to your mom? Picture her reaction. How would it feel getting to stay on the football team? What would your coaches say, if they knew you were on the honor roll? What will you have to do to make it happen? What will you commit yourself to every day?

I saw Guy close his eyes and picture himself as an honors student. That smile crept back onto his face. The next semester, he made honor roll for the first time ever. Guy's journey through middle and high school wasn't easy. But he never gave up, and he achieved his dream of being the first member of his family to go to college. Today, he's a proud husband and father, and after a successful career as a paralegal, he and his wife started a business that provides transportation services to inner-city community members in Boston. His vision made it happen.

The Adventure Begins

Sometimes, it was easier to teach creative visualization to a scholar like Guy than it was to use it myself. Graduation loomed, and I was alone and afraid. BELL had started as a group volunteer project, but my friends were moving on, and I was going to have to be the one to turn it into a fully functioning organization. I had secretly hoped that my friend Drew, my closest partner in building BELL, might change his mind and agree to launch the nonprofit with me. But Drew was moving on to a job as a public defender, like he'd planned. I struggled to accept his decision, but I knew Drew had never promised me anything. I just had trouble facing the future on my own. I knew that building BELL was my dream, but I also knew that I had absolutely no idea what I was doing. The first leader I needed to build was myself.

CHAPTER 6

Learning to Lead

Echoing Green

"So," the man in the suit said, pausing to look down at the papers in front of him, "tell us about… the BELL Foundation, Building Enterprises for Learning and Living."

It was the summer of 1993, I was fresh out of law school, and I had made it into the final round. There were thirty-six organizations competing for just twelve Echoing Green fellowships. Back then, Echoing Green was a new type of foundation. It focused on helping young leaders get their socially conscious projects up and running. Each of the twelve fellows selected would receive $25,000 a year for two years, plus assistance and support from Echoing

Green. I just had to ace this presentation and impress the five blank-faced professionals staring me down from the other side of the conference table.

I had spent the whole day listening to my competition make their presentations. The other nonprofits had business plans and clear, rehearsed answers to questions about theory of change and long-term sustainability. I hadn't thought through our budget, our staffing plan, or our metrics for long-term growth.

But it was too late for all that. Without any funding, a detailed business plan would be pointless. I needed money now.

"BELL was started by a small group of Black law students at Harvard Law School," I began, trying to sound self-assured. "The purpose of the organization is to provide programs to help strengthen the Black community."

I knew I had to get at least three panel members on my side. I scanned the faces at the table, looking for hints of sympathy or interest.

"We operate three core programs," I explained. *Three is a good number,* I thought. I hoped it sounded impressive.

"The BELL After School Program runs educational programs for elementary school children. The Young Prophets Program provides mentoring for pregnant teen girls, and the Charles Ogletree Scholarship Fund grants college scholarships to high school seniors from low-income families."

I went on, trying to add as much detail as I could without giving hard financial numbers I couldn't back up.

Ed, the lead panelist, took off his glasses and rubbed the bridge of his nose. Rumor had it that he had eviscerated several finalists and even walked out on a few presentations. At least he was still in the room.

"Thank you for your presentation, Earl," he said carefully. "You're clearly passionate about the work you do."

I had trouble reading his tone. Was he congratulating me, or being condescending?

"I have some concerns about the number of programs you're looking to include here," Ed continued. "First, I don't understand how they're all related. Second, I think your lack of programmatic focus will ultimately undermine the success of all of them."

I shifted in my seat.

"Which of these programs is actually important to you?" Ed asked.

You need the money, Earl, I reminded myself, willing my calm, professional self to come to the surface.

"All of our programs are important," I told him. "But right now, we're most invested in our after-school program and scholarship fund."

"But all of our programs, um, they're all led by young adults," I added, trying to stay alive, "giving back to the Black community—and ultimately focused on children and education. That's the link."

Ed was curt. "It sounds like you want to be a clearinghouse for Black student volunteers."

Another member of the panel jumped in. "I see the link, Earl," he said gently, "but you may want to launch one program and pilot it. Then roll out the others at the appropriate time."

I winced at the words "appropriate time," but I could tell the panelist was on my side. I nodded and agreed and did my best to answer the rest of the panel's questions. Later that day, I got the news that Echoing Green had chosen not to move forward with my application. They thought BELL had too many programs and not enough forethought, and that my chance of success was minimal.

Chance of success was minimal. That stung.

I knew I couldn't give up so easily. That evening, I got in touch with the panelist who had spoken on my behalf.

I made my case again, just to him: I had been nervous and "off" at my presentation. I was a huge admirer of Echoing Green's work and needed the help they provided. It would mean so much to me to be able to benefit from their training and resources, even if I couldn't get the financial benefits of a grant.

The panelist listened, and he told me he'd see what he could do. A few days later, the committee came back with some news. They would award BELL a one-time grant of $12,500 to build the organization, and I would be welcome to apply again next year. I remember getting off the phone with the committee and feeling like I'd taken my first breath after minutes underwater. That $12,500 ended up being BELL's entire first-year operating budget. I don't know how we would have survived without it.

That Echoing Green experience taught me the value of preparation. There would be no more bluffing through my presentations if I wanted to be taken seriously by donors. And when I was able to step back and reflect, I realized that Ed had been half right. BELL needed focus. I put our plans for the Young Prophets on hold and set to work building up our after-school program.

Six Months of Silence

That summer of 1993, every move BELL made felt crucial. After Echoing Green's rejection, I submitted over one hundred proposals. Most were for grants between $5,000 and $25,000. Some requests were for as much as $100,000. The budgets I drew up were clearly the work of a novice. So were my mission statements and my theory of change. I claimed that, with funder support, BELL would be able serve 1,000 scholars—it would have taken $1.5 million to deliver on that promise, not the $250,000 annual budget that I forecasted. I was winging it, and it showed.

Looking back, I must have seemed crazy to the people around me. I was running on creative visualization, Tony Robbins audiotapes, Napoleon Hill's *Think and Grow Rich*, and my borrowed copy of *How to Fundraise*, keeping the faith that the win BELL needed was just around the corner.

I was used to calling on my parents when I needed some good advice and a morale boost. By that summer, they were frustrated with my decisions. During one of my long, challenging calls, my mom finally snapped at me—or at least as much as she could "snap."

"At some point you just have to get a job!" I could hear her exasperation. "Earl, you're a Harvard Law School graduate. You could be earning a six-figure salary right now."

"Mom." I was losing my patience too. "I chose my passion…"

"The *only* reason that you are able to pursue your *passion*," my mom said, with a sarcasm that was uncharacteristic of her, "is because your father and I are helping to pay your law school debt and allowing you to live rent free in the condo."

My dad was silent on the other end of the line. He was never a fan of conflict.

"If you don't want to support me, you don't have to," I bit back. This was a total bluff—I knew that they would always support me.

My dad cleared his throat.

"We're just saying, Earl, sometimes you have to face reality. You could work at a law firm and do this on the side."

"You can't do what I want to do *on the side*!" I retorted. I couldn't believe my mom and dad were acting like BELL was some kind of hobby.

"How much money have you raised so far?" my mother asked, trying to bring me back down to Earth.

I tried to explain to her that raising money was a process, that it took time to craft proposals and build relationships in the philanthropic community, that one breakthrough was all I needed to keep the momentum.

"Sounds like a lot of excuses to me," my mom said flatly.

I don't remember the rest of the conversation. I do remember that I didn't call my parents again for another six months. If I couldn't convince them that BELL was a serious organization, and that I was a good fundraiser, I would show them instead.

I felt lonelier and more determined than ever. Building BELL was taking all of my emotional energy and I could not battle my mother's lack of belief. I deeply missed my parents, but even our disagreement couldn't make me doubt their love. I knew they would be back. For now, if my parents weren't ready to support the mission, it was time for me to find someone who would.

My First Partners

We were lucky to have a wonderful staff of after-school volunteers, mostly Black undergrad and law students who did fantastic work with our scholars. But I needed someone who understood BELL's educational vision and had the expertise to take the program to the next level. My old friend Motty recommended Arlene Hudson. I was so impressed by her when we met. She had grown up in Jamaica, in the old British school system, and it showed in her perfect posture and calm, regal air. Her passion for education, and the welfare of Black children, was unmatched, but she wasn't one of those teachers who goes in for kids' games and goofy antics. She was always Ms. Hudson, and she insisted that I at least make the scholars call me Mr. Earl. Even with her serious, no-nonsense ways, all the scholars loved her, and she loved them right back. And she could do everything—education, training, marketing, human resources.

It was the two of us, Arlene at the kitchen table and me on the couch in our office, which happened to be my condo, for those first few years. We worked hard and butted heads, but we always made up in the end. I'd say she was the sister I never had, but I have four, and Arlene and I had that same frank familiarity from day one. I never left a conversation with Arlene not knowing exactly what she thought. Late night after late night, argument after argument, we built a curriculum for the after-school program. It was Arlene's idea to build a series of lessons around the six days of Kwanzaa, so that our scholars would learn the principles of African American community along with their academic lessons.

And long before *summer learning loss* was an accepted piece of educational wisdom, Arlene noticed that our scholars were losing precious ground during the summer months. They came back to the programs in the fall with a dent in the confidence they'd cultivated, and without many of the gains in reading and math they'd worked so hard on.

One day, I was lying on the couch, giving myself a headache with budget numbers, when Arlene walked in. She stopped in front of the couch, peering down at me until I put away my papers and sat upright.

"All great companies have multiple products," she said, skipping hello, "and we are missing the boat by just having one."

I didn't know what she was getting at, but when Arlene had an idea, it was best to stop and listen.

"It's time to expand BELL," she said. "We need a summer program."

"Think about it," she said. "We can have a healthy breakfast and lunch for the scholars. We can use the mornings for reading, writing, and math, and then we have the afternoons free for enrichment classes like art and drama."

As she talked, I started to picture it. A place for scholars to keep growing and supporting each other, with mentorship and good meals. But what about their summers?

"I like it, Arlene," I said. "But how are we going to keep it fun for the scholars?"

"Earl!" She looked fed up. "You are always thinking about how to make it fun!"

"It's about *learning*," she said, drawing out the word. "Sometimes it is fun, and sometimes it is not fun. But our babies *will* learn how to read and write!"

"I know, Arlene…"

"But to answer your question," she interrupted, "we'll have afternoon activities the students enjoy, and we'll have the college mentors spend time with them throughout the day. And we will have service projects on Friday, just like we do now. *That* is enough to make a Friday fun."

I couldn't argue with that. And so, the BELL Accelerated Learning Summer Program, now known as Summer Advantage, launched the next year.

Growing Pains

In 1995, BELL moved into the 200-square-foot office space at Cambridge College that would be our home base for the next four years. We expanded our services to two new schools and opened the summer program, and soon we were serving hundreds of scholars in the Boston area. Our salaries were $20,000 per year; no one had health insurance; we had buggy Mac computers, none of which were linked together. Even so, the core of the mission was working. We were helping more and more scholars every year, and we were building a reputation as a nonprofit with big ideas and talented staff. I didn't want us to remain solely a Boston organization; it was time to take BELL nationwide.

In order to effectively replicate a business model in a new region, you need several important things. The most important are a structured and proven program model; strong financial health, including start-up capital for the new region; the ability to train staff to implement the model; the political clout to successfully enter a new market; and a strong leader.

When I decided to expand BELL to New York City in 1996, I had exactly one of those things: Arlene. She was moving to New York, and that was the push I needed to decide on expansion. It was a gamble that pushed us into debt, but with so many scholars who needed our programming, I knew we needed to act boldly.

In 1997, our staff grew from two to six. It was my first time serving as a full-time boss, and that year was a tremendous struggle. I worked harder when we had a staff of six then when it was just the two of us. Back then, I hired people based on not much more than gut feeling. I considered each new employee a gift from the universe, convinced that the mission would attract the right people to us at the right time. Predictably, sometimes that worked out, and often it didn't. My commitment to staying positive helped move BELL forward, but we also had our fair share of employee dysfunction. The first time I ever had to fire a staff member, I ended up turning our termination meeting into an impromptu therapy session and pep talk. I let her stay on, but our heart-to-heart had the opposite effect of what I'd hoped for: her job performance got worse, and so did her morale. I watched her get more and more checked out of the job and had to fire her again a few months later. It took me a long time to learn how to balance empathy with effective boundaries.

That year marked the beginning of a long quest for me. As a leader, I had to learn how to balance two opposing duties: cultivating the optimism we needed to move forward and maintaining the realism we needed to tackle serious problems. I struggled for years to learn how to communicate, when to share and when to keep silent.

At the time, my theory was that if you give people positive news, you bring more good energy, more momentum and, therefore, more positive news. If you tell people bad news, the opposite occurs. Funders lose confidence, staff and volunteer morale goes down, and partners pull out. I knew that part of my job as a leader was being BELL's biggest and most committed cheerleader. But I frustrated the members of the board, not to mention our funding partners, when I didn't pay enough attention to the very real limitations of our cash flow. Ultimately, my desire to expand past what our financial resources could support— and my need to keep pushing the good news—led to a crisis. I saw the problem coming, and I didn't raise the flag in time.

And that problem came crashing into us in the form of a $400,000 debt. I could spin it as the price of progress, or as a ticking time bomb that the organization would have to deal with later. In the end, it was a mix of both.

Management by Miracle

As BELL got bigger, I began to spend less time in the classroom and more time in boardrooms and on planes. I was facing the paradox of the nonprofit leader: you start a nonprofit because you're passionate about helping others, connecting with them in tangible, meaningful ways. But if you're lucky enough to grow your organization, eventually you become a CEO, not a service provider. I missed working with children, the daily inspirations of their creativity and resilience. But BELL needed me to make myself into a skilled businessman. I was struggling to learn how to better manage BELL without losing touch with why I had begun this journey in the first place.

Those first few years were often difficult. But amidst all the self-doubt, there was one thing that I knew I was doing right: finding good people. Leadership can feel lonely, but being a leader is never about going it alone. My family had taught me a lesson I had seen reinforced over and over in the most important moments of my life: at the shelter at Luther Place, in that classroom in Jamaica, in the car with my friends on the way home from Roxbury. A leader's true strength comes from his relationships with others: learning from their gifts, relying on their talents.

In the early days, my best moments as a leader came when I was able to find the people whose insight and support helped us keep the lights on. George & George at State Street Foundation, who took a risk on me as a young social entrepreneur; my old suitemate Chris's mom, Gilda Wray at the Charles Hayden Foundation, who saw our potential from the outset; Paul Grogan at the Boston Foundation, whose support led to the support of so many others; and Sylvia Johnson and Klare Shaw at Hyams who I think just wanted me, as a young and passionate Black male leader, to succeed. Our earliest donors and supporters (and my beloved family) swooped in to help us through the years of shoestring budgets when I didn't know just where the next payroll would be coming from. Even in our most uncertain moments, part of me kept faith that my team and the people supporting BELL could help us make it through somehow. One of our first partners, George at New Profit Inc., used to call my leadership style "management by miracle." But he, my team, and all of our earliest partners were the miracles.

In 1996, the Charles Hayden Foundation demonstrated their belief in our work by giving a generous grant to our New York program. This was the perfect opportunity for me to spend a little time with our New York scholars. I decided to pay them a visit, to thank them and to celebrate. I walked into a class of thirty eager and talented third graders, ready to share the good news.

"Do you remember me?" I asked a girl sitting in the front.

"You're Mr. Fallon!" she shouted.

"Exactly—Mr. Phalen. You did a very good job remembering. It shows me that you, that all of you, really pay attention. You are very good listeners and all very, very smart."

The scholars were beaming.

"The last time I was here we had a visitor. Do you remember why?"

"Oh!!! Oh!!!" The scholars straightened in their seats to get their hands up higher in the air.

"Wow, I love your energy. Okay," I said to a patient but eager boy in the middle, "please share with the group."

"The visitor," the scholar started confidently, "came here to visit with us, see the work that we do, and give us money."

"That's exactly right," I replied. "And can you guess how much the funder gave us?"

"One hundred dollars!" said one scholar, as though that was the largest sum of money imaginable.

"Close," I responded, "but it was more than that."

"A thousand dollars," guessed another scholar.

"I think they gave us a zillion dollars," said another.

"Well, those are all great guesses," I responded encouragingly. "Because she met you and was so impressed by all of your hard work and effort, the foundation gave us fifty thousand dollars."

The room exploded with cheers. The scholars were so excited that *they* had helped raise that much money.

"It's very exciting," I said, calming the room down a little. I noticed one scholar raise her hand.

"What are we going to do with the money?" she asked.

"What are we going to do…" I repeated, almost to myself.

And then, I thought of the Super Bowl commercials that were popular at the time, and without thinking I imitated the athletes and raised my arms, exclaiming, "We're going to Disney World!"

The room erupted in excitement, thirty children crying out with pure, unadulterated joy. I realized I had made an enormous mistake.

"No, no," I said quickly, "I was just kidding."

The energy in the room deflated like a popped balloon. The scholars looked at each other, confused. The adults looked at me with the kind of stunned disappointment you never want to see on another person's face.

"We're going to use the money to provide BELL After School to other scholars like you," I explained. "Won't that be great, to invite more scholars to come learn like you do?"

The looks on the scholars' faces told me that they didn't think that was all that great at all. Some of the more easygoing scholars agreed it was nice to help others, but the damage had been done.

Arlene lit into me on the way home. How dare I play with our scholars' emotions like that, what on earth was I thinking, did I think I could just say any old thing to our scholars with no consequences, and on and on. It was a lecture I knew I deserved, but there was nothing to be done. I couldn't unsay what I had said, any more than I could actually take all those kids to Disney World.

Unless…

Six months after that classroom visit, BELL raised donations from some of our most dedicated funders and took a total of 150 scholars, parents, siblings, tutors, and staff on a three-day, two-night trip to Walt Disney World. I got to see the joy on those scholars' faces all over again. I'll never forget the jumps and cheers the moment we reached the gates of the park. The entire BELL family had time to bond and relax, a rare and precious opportunity in those hectic early years.

For me, that trip was a kind of miracle, the miracle we needed. It showed me that there were people willing to invest in our vision, even when our dreams took us to far-away places. I'll always be grateful to our earliest donors, teams, and champions, without whom we could have never built BELL. And it was a reminder that no matter how far my work took me from the scholars, I could still share in their growth and their joy.

Two Awards

The next year, we got some good news—proof that our own growth as an organization hadn't gone unrecognized. In 1997, BELL was one of sixteen organizations chosen for the President's Service Award. We owed our nomination to Marian Heard, the head of the United Way of Massachusetts Bay and one of our biggest advocates. I couldn't believe we'd come this far, this quickly. It was like a sign from the universe that despite our money worries and our growing pains, we were doing something right.

I went to the awards gala with some of my staff, but I discouraged my parents from attending. By this time, they had seen the work we were doing at BELL and were my biggest cheerleaders—I don't regret much, but I will always regret not having them in that auditorium with me. (Years later, when I was honored at the BET Awards, I made sure my nieces Veronica and Jordan could be there too.)

At the President's Service Awards, over 2,500 people had shown up, and the first seats were filled by some of the most powerful and well-known celebrities, athletes, politicians, and businesspeople in the country.

Oprah Winfrey was at the podium, commanding the crowd's attention.

"The President's Service Awards were created in 1982 to recognize outstanding individuals and organizations in volunteer service," she began. After a short speech, she gave the podium to President Clinton, who was to recognize several of the honorees. I struggled to take in what he was saying, overwhelmed by the star power in the room, until I heard him start to say my name.

"Earl Martin Phalen…"

The leader of the most powerful nation in the world is talking about me.

"…has given hundreds of African American young adults the chance to be role models and tutors to inner-city elementary school students throughout the greater Boston area. Under their tutelage, those children are thriving. Their futures are brighter, and therefore so are ours. Tonight we honor Earl Martin Phalen for his remarkable contribution to our American community."

I felt like I was floating towards the podium. As I walked to the president, I looked at each member in the front row—President and Mrs. Ford, the mayor of Philadelphia and his wife, President and Mrs. Carter, First Lady Nancy Reagan, and General and Mrs. Colin Powell. As my eyes met General Powell's, I bowed, as a signal of my deep respect and admiration. He and his wife smiled.

"Thank you, President Clinton," He shook my hand like a brother, and my nervousness evaporated.

"Thank you, Earl," President Clinton said, and I spent a moment in the high beams of that famous charm. "We appreciate all that you do for the children of the nation."

It was an incredible moment. In times of doubt, I have often revisited that minute on the podium. But when I think back to that time in BELL's history, there's another awards ceremony I remember even more clearly.

In the spring of 1996, we gathered together in Cambridge to celebrate the five recipients of the Charles Ogletree Scholarship Fund. Our first honoree, Deeqo Jibril, came to the stage and smiled shyly at all of us in the audience—the staff at BELL, her family, and the families of the other recipients.

"I'd like to begin by thanking God," she said, in a soft but clear voice.

Deeqo shared her story. She had been born in Somalia and grew up in a country torn by a vicious civil war. At twelve years old, she came to US with her mother; her father and two brothers, who had hoped to immigrate later, lost their lives in the violence. Deeqo and her mother had to start over on their own.

"It has been a struggle," Deeqo said, "but my mother worked so hard to make sure that there was food on the table and that I had access to a good education."

Deeqo paused as her eyes filled with tears; everyone else in the room was either in tears or holding them back. Her experience was ours, and ours hers. We knew the strength and courage it took to be where she was. We knew the love she felt for her mother and father and siblings. And we knew the sacrifices that went into providing this opportunity. As she left the podium, we all stood up, clapping for Deeqo and cheering on her future. Deeqo graduated from college in Boston and has been a community organizer for over twenty years. She has worked to protect Bostonians facing housing insecurity, and she created her own local mall in Roxbury, featuring and promoting African small businesses. Today, she works for Boston's mayor in the Office of Economic Development.

The President's Service Award was a tremendous honor. But getting to celebrate with scholars like Deeqo has been the greatest privilege of my life. My own moment in the spotlight was a recognition of how far we'd come; Deeqo's was a reminder that no matter what, we needed to keep going.

CHAPTER 7

A Mission, Not a Business

Stay Black

There was a bar right around the corner from BELL's office in Dorchester, a Boston Irish pub called the Blarney Stone. The team would often meet there after work on Fridays, for a chance to unwind and welcome in the weekend. We would get there after five and watch the regulars roll in, then the latecomers, then the partyers. Evening was just turning into night when I saw an attractive Black woman looking at me from across the room. She was in her mid-forties, in a blue dress and gold earrings that showed off her long neck. I walked up to the bar and stood next to her chair. She smiled and put out her hand.

"You're Earl with the BELL Foundation, aren't you?"

It was just BELL, but I wasn't about to correct her.

"Yes, I am."

"You do great work," she told me.

I looked down at the floor, feeling suddenly shy even as I basked in her attention.

"Earl," she said, a little nervousness in her voice. "This might not be my place to say, but I hope that you will stay Black."

I didn't know how to respond. She looked me up and down, registering my surprise.

"It's just that—" She paused, choosing her words carefully. "There are so many social service organizations and nonprofits and charities, but there are so few that are led by *us*."

"I know you'll grow," she continued, "and sometimes when you grow, the complexion of the organization changes. I just want to encourage you to *keep it Black*."

We looked at each other for a moment without speaking, the noise of the jukebox drowning out the silence between us.

"Thanks for your feedback," I said, feeling a little like I was pitching to an investor. "Our work is so challenging that I always look for the most talented people, and sometimes…"

I stopped. She looked me in the eyes with a mix of cynicism, respect, and something I couldn't name.

"I will never let us move away from being a Black organization," I told her.

But in many ways, I already had.

When I started BELL, I drafted up a master plan, in the spirit of Malcolm X's plan for the Organization of African American Unity. My vision was to use BELL to advocate for the empowerment, health, and success of the Black community. The plan broke down the concrete steps an organization like BELL could take to realize that vision. Self-Defense was the first—I wanted to build communities where Black people felt safe, and reduce our risk of gun violence—followed by Education, Politics-Economics, Social and Health, and Culture. It was a private document, a reminder to myself about the breadth of the mission. BELL was meant to be about so much more than offering educational services. I imagined us branching out into political advocacy, public health work, cultural representation, family and social services, all in the name of creating systems that help Black people uplift themselves. I wanted us to have financial counselors, prenatal care nurses, local and national lobbies, career services and counseling.

Officially, BELL's mission statement was:

"One day BELL will educate over 100,000 children, young adults and parents annually. BELL will help children master the basic academic and social skills needed to excel in school and life and will help build strong Black and Latino communities with well-educated children, socially conscious young adults, and engaged parents."

In practice, that goal was more than enough of a challenge. And if we were going to rise to that challenge, we needed as many allies as possible. I treasured the work of colleagues like Arlene, Tiffany, Marsha, Pam, Ayana, Darnell, Collette, Imari, and Mark, who not only understood the principles of Black self-determination but lived them deeply and beautifully. But at the end of the day, we deeply value all of the scholars who trust us with their learning, and a good teacher, regardless of background, is a priceless gift to the scholars she teaches. Black and brown children are especially underserved by our school system, but our job was to educate all of our scholars, and to find the best people available to ensure that we fulfilled our mission.

The woman at the Blarney Stone had said something out loud that I had grappled with in the privacy of my own thoughts: *sometimes when you grow, the complexion of the organization changes.* I believed, and still believe, that at the end of the day, doing the best we can for children is more important to me than leading a Black organization.

But I knew there was an invisible line somewhere that I had to be careful not to cross. If we couldn't stay Black, we would need to stay true: true to the children in our care, true to the reasons we were doing this in the first place.

Is this my dream?

"Earl," that famous Austrian accent, with its clipped, macho confidence, came over the phone. "My assistant said that you called."

Back then, Arnold Schwarzenegger was quick to return my calls. In 1995, the Terminator had become executive commissioner of Inner City Games (ICG), an organization that provided after-school athletic programs for disadvantaged youth. By 2002, the organization was operating with a $27 million budget and worked with 500,000 children in fifteen cities. They were looking for a CEO to take their vision to the next level. I was one of two finalists.

That first meeting with Arnold and his team could not have gone better. He laughed at my getting-to-know-you jokes and gave us his focused, straight-to-camera stare while we outlined a vision of the future ICG and BELL could have together. I talked about what we'd been able to accomplish in BELL's ten years of operation: they were especially impressed by our move to Washington, DC, a market ICG hadn't been able to penetrate. I was confident and at ease. It felt natural to be in the room with these people, to be the kind of nonprofit leader they looked up to. I could tell Arnold was a decisive man. By the end of our pitch, he was nodding along, a satisfied smile on his face.

"OK," he said, "I don't need to hear any more. When you speak, it's like music to my ears."

That was music to my ears too. A little later, his second-in-command, Tim, pulled me aside to update me on the search committee's progress.

"Bring your party hat, Earl," said Tim, with a car salesman's oily smile. "They just want to meet you one more time and finalize the terms."

About a week later, the call came in: Arnold wanted me to be ICG's new CEO.

The offer came at a time of crisis for BELL. We had expanded too quickly: the program in New York had taken off in terms of enrollment but was struggling financially, and while we were up and running in DC, we had locked ourselves into an unsustainable lease. Years of financial ups and downs had taken their toll.

Our wonderful early backers had done so much to get us off the ground but expanding the organization had meant expanding our funding base. We had entered the world of big philanthropy, of organizations that wrote checks for millions rather than thousands of dollars. These large foundations and funds expected oversight over the projects they invested in. And some of them were losing patience with my habit of getting out of budget crises by the skin of my teeth.

If I accepted ICG's CEO offer, I would integrate BELL into ICG's existing structure. In exchange for $250,000 a year each for our programs in Boston and DC, BELL would move some of its New York staff to ICG's offices and focus on bringing our curriculum, with its proven record of academic excellence, to ICG. For years, we'd been dreaming of expanding BELL nationally. ICG could bring this dream—or a version of it—to life. We'd help deepen ICG's programming, transforming it from a nationally linked group of sports camps to a comprehensive and rigorous after-school program that could uplift thousands of scholars and help them get to college and beyond.

At least, that was the plan from our end. It was difficult to pin Tim down on the details. When I tried to talk to him about how ICG would support and integrate BELL's programs, he was evasive, noncommittal.

While I tried to imagine what my future as ICG's CEO could look like, the pressure from some of our funders intensified. After one of our biggest donors found out I was considering merging BELL with ICG, I received a long, stern letter from their CEO.

We sincerely hope, the CEO wrote, addressing me like a child she'd caught sneaking out after curfew, *that the first and overriding consideration for your current discussions is BELL's best interest, and the fulfillment of its stated mission "to raise the educational achievements and life opportunities of low income children."*

I had to resist the urge to tear the letter up. *She* had the audacity to question my commitment. But that, for the most part, is philanthropy. It's a very white, very wealthy world. A small group of people write big checks to support the causes they care about: they want to help, but many also want control, because they feel they know better. I was tired of being treated like a marionette by these all-knowing so-called philanthropists, all of them with their own agendas and none of them with our vision or even an ounce of our passion.

And yet, ICG was a white-led organization: one whose budget dwarfed ours and whose reach was five times what my wildest dreams could imagine for BELL's growth. They had a policy presence, a national brand, and heavy hitters like Yankees owner George Steinbrenner on the board. If I could harness their influence in service of BELL's mission, I might be able to accomplish great things. But I knew that becoming ICG's CEO meant that I was giving up some of my control over BELL's direction, over my vision. A future without ICG meant more struggles for funding and a nearly unreachable path to impacting the millions of children who needed us. A future with ICG might mean compromising on BELL's deep commitment to high-quality, high-impact programming.

I spent weeks polling friends, mentors—everyone whose opinion I valued. I was tempted to tap strangers on the shoulder and ask if they had a moment to consider the pros and cons. I sat down with my close friend and colleague Tuck, who I trusted to think through every facet of a problem. He gave it to me straight.

"It sounds like if you take this position," he said, "it's going to hurt BELL and hurt the scholars that we're currently serving."

He took a breath.

"And…it also sounds like this is an amazing opportunity for you. If I were you, I would go for it."

I thanked Tuck, knowing he was right. This CEO job could be wonderful for me, but I also knew that I wasn't going to do what was best for my BELL scholars. But if I had to make a choice, how could I tell where my interests ended and my scholars' interests began? Where was that invisible line?

I found myself back at my parents' house on Sunday morning, having the breakfast conversations that served as my anchor. I told them about the feeling of being pulled in many directions at once, away from the scholars and towards stable, increased funding. I told them what my brother Jimmy had said in one of our phone calls—that I would never have more power with ICG than I did at that moment, when I was still their most desirable candidate.

"Earl," my mother said, "trying to please everyone is not leadership."

She looked at me, to see if her words had sunken in.

"You've given your entire life to BELL," she continued. "No one knows more about what the organization needs than you. No one knows more about what BELL does for children and can do for communities than you."

My father looked proudly at her, then nodded his head in agreement.

"I know that leadership isn't easy," she said, "but you have *always* been a leader."

I treasured her words, and I knew she was right. I asked ICG for a firm commitment to implementing BELL's programming: when I couldn't get it, I walked away from the offer.

After the ICG offer disappeared for good, Professor Ogletree sent a note to BELL's board. I still have my copy.

It is important that you know how deeply we appreciate your personal, professional, and financial sacrifices for BELL. The organization would not exist, and could not be sustained, without your unequivocal leadership, he wrote, with his typical generosity of spirit. I treasured his vote of confidence. At the time, it was one of the few I felt like I still had. But I had my mother's words, and I had my master plan, and I had my wonderful teammates, our early supporters, the scholars, and all that we had achieved so far. And that was enough.

Do Right Man

So at BELL, we stuck to the original plan: growth and expansion, our way. We kept the program in New York, and we expanded into Baltimore in 2003. I was optimistic about the future: I had reconnected with then Senator Obama, who introduced the STEP UP bill in 2005. The bill relied on our work on summer learning loss to secure $100 million in funding for summer enrichment programs like BELL's. It was an incredible moment for us, an acknowledgement that our impact was being seen and felt. And it brought some unexpected publicity with it.

By 2006, we had served 20,000 scholars. That year, *Essence* magazine featured me in their Do Right Man list—fifty eligible Black bachelors who did good work in the community. I got a photo in the magazine and a brief feature on my work with BELL. They asked each of us what we loved about Black women, printed our answers, and encouraged interested women to write to us. This time I was in a suit and button-down instead of a wetsuit, and I gave the camera a steady gaze. I was featured alongside Hollywood heartthrobs like Idris Elba, Michael Ealy, and Reggie Bush, but I still got about 1,000 emails from interested women. I answered the ones who caught my eye, and a correspondence with a stylish professional in Virginia led to a relationship. We agreed to be monogamous, even though I wasn't sure I was ready. I never meant to hurt her—it felt like it just happened—but I ended up seeing someone else while we were still long-distance, and she found out. Our relationship limped along a little while longer, but though I tried to make amends for the pain I'd caused, it never really recovered.

Tiffany, my COO, shook her head at my adventures as an *Essence* bachelor. "You may be a Do Good Man," she told me once, smiling wryly, "but you're definitely not a Do Right Man."

She would know. After all, she was my ex-fiancée.

I met Tiffany at BELL, when she became a teacher in our programs and, later, the youngest (and, she pointed out, the best) site manager in our organization's history. She had grown up in a family that had had everything except money, and her strong values and love for children shone through in everything she did. She was a popular honors student at the suburban school her district bused her to, and by twenty-eight years old she had already earned her PhD in Educational Research, Management, and Evaluation. She was brilliant, fearless, determined, and kind. She believed in our mission, and she never hesitated to challenge me if she thought I wasn't doing what was best for the scholars. When our engagement fell apart, I had to ask myself what it was I was looking for that I hadn't already found.

I got a clue some years later, when another girlfriend asked me to go to a few sessions with her therapist. It wasn't the first time I had seen a counselor. Back in law school, I had talked to a psychologist when the basketball league competitions got tense, and that old feeling that I would choke in a crisis came back. The psychologist had extended my three free sessions into a period of several months, and we had practiced visualization techniques, emotional control. Of course, I had been stressed about much more than basketball, and strengthening my visualization practice had helped me on and off the court. But I had never told him what I was about to tell this therapist.

She was an older woman, wrapped in a shawl and sitting in a scuffed armchair. She seemed totally focused on me, but her face stayed still and placid as I told her my story.

I would meet an interesting, attractive woman, and we would hit it off. Things were always fun and easy at first: the spark of chemistry, the excitement of new courtship. Part of me wanted to nurture those sparks into a steady, long-term commitment, a slow-burning fire that would add warmth and security to my life. The other part of me got restless in relationships, always wondering what else was out there. I wanted new sparks, new energy. And no matter how wonderful the woman or how strong our connection, the fire would go out.

And I wanted to know if my secret fear was true.

"I think it might be because I'm adopted," I said. "The problems with women."

The therapist gave a slow nod.

"Issues with commitment are very common, Earl," she said. "And most people aren't adopted. Tell me more about the connection you see between the two."

She scribbled in her notepad as I told her about the two foster homes I lived in before I was two years old. I gave her my hazy memories of saying goodbye to my social worker Fran, who I later learned had considered adopting me herself.

"And then you bonded with your parents," she pointed out. "So you may have made four or five strong bonds by the time you were two years old."

She paused, giving me a moment to think.

"What meaning do you think you ascribed to these experiences?"

I didn't know what to tell her. What meaning does a two-year-old *ascribe* to anything? But I came to understand what she was saying. I had loved each of these people the way a small child does, helplessly and completely. They had seemed to love me back; but they had left me, and I had had to start over, again and again. Now I was the one who drew people in, earning their love and trust only to push it away.

I felt a wave of compassion for that little boy who kept everyone at a distance, terrified of being hurt again. I was still angry at the grown man who had surely inflicted enough of his own hurt already. I left that session and walked into the biting Boston winter air. I walked aimlessly for a while, feeling muddled and clear at the same time. The therapist had helped me understand something about my past, but it wasn't that simple. You can't break a pattern just by looking at it. The girlfriend who had asked me to go to therapy broke up with me three months later. She had gotten tired of waiting for me to change.

A Mission, Not a Business

On the upside, I had very little free time to dwell on my romantic troubles. I was on the road, working one-hundred-hour weeks, trying to get the money and the resources to keep BELL going.

With the help of my team, I got meetings with a large array of ultrawealthy philanthropists, captains of industry who needed to figure out how to make an impact in the world with the fortunes they'd amassed. I found myself face-to-face with a modern tycoon, a man whose early investment in the television business had made him a billionaire. Now he had the time and the means to give generously to any cause that mattered to him, and he took a special interest in K-12 education.

We met in a drab, concrete-heavy Boston office building. Like a man accustomed to making big decisions, he cut to the chase.

"Why do you want to expand?"

I was tired of that peremptory, pop-quiz tone. Still, I was prepared.

"Because we have something that works for children, and the need is so great."

"Well, you can't build a business based on need," he said, winding up for his lecture. "Growing with quality is incredibly expensive and incredibly hard."

"Well, you grew quickly," I shot back. "Why did you want to expand the TV business?"

"You're comparing apples and oranges," he said. "I've seen it over and over again. So many nonprofits try to grow and do nothing but erode the quality of what they had."

"I'm still confused," I said, even though I wasn't. "Nonprofits and for-profits are both businesses. If there are a set number of steps that a business needs to take in order to grow responsibly, and we are able to define and execute those steps, then the tax designation of the business is irrelevant."

Now I was winding up.

"Why would giving every American home two hundred TV channels be more important than giving every American child a quality education?"

I don't remember how he replied to that. I've had so many versions of this frustrating conversation that they all start to blend together. Somehow, I could meet with the greatest business minds in the country, and still not come away with a single piece of advice on how to make my own business better. If the issue is that most nonprofits don't have the necessary resources to scale, why can't we talk about that? If it's that nonprofits lack a sustainable economic engine, isn't that a problem worth tackling? If the concern is that nonprofit workers are inexperienced, or inefficient, or implement faulty systems, why can't that be addressed?

We tell our children, our scholars, that despite lives lived among extreme poverty, violence, drugs, dysfunctional schools, and sometimes dysfunctional homes, that they should never stop believing that they can graduate from college, pursue their passions, and live healthy and fulfilled lives. Yet we, with wealth, leadership, and talent at our fingertips, limit our vision so severely. We act like it's a virtue to stay small and conservative, that we're better off not pushing too hard.

The billionaire was right about one thing. At the end of the day, BELL wasn't a business, not really. It was a mission. Every day that goes by is a day millions of children are denied the education they deserve. It's not about having the best systems or making an impressive expansion plan. It's definitely not about making money. It's about giving our scholars something they deserve, something that's long past due already. There is no expansion plan too ambitious when we are talking about the hearts and minds of the five million children currently attending abysmal schools in the US. And there is absolutely no time to waste.

Whenever I'm tempted to stay small or act cautiously, I think of all my heroes: the brave members of the Montgomery Bus Boycott, who sacrificed their jobs, the security of their families, and their lives to provide the opportunities I take for granted today. I think of Harriet Tubman, who freed herself from bondage but was willing to go back South again, and again, and again. I try to draw on some fraction of their dedication and their strength. I remind myself who all of this is for.

CHAPTER 8

Coming Full Circle

Starting PLA

I stepped down from BELL in 2008; with Tiffany as CEO, though, I knew that BELL would continue to thrive. It was my old friend Motty who gave me a push towards a new adventure. He called me about an organization called the Mind Trust—they were offering fellowships to people who could improve public education in Indianapolis and nationwide. I didn't know anything about Indianapolis, but I did know how many school districts nationwide were getting it wrong when it came to summer learning. Indiana was spending $450 per student on half-day summer school programs that clashed with working parents' schedules and didn't offer comprehensive learning. I knew that for just $600 per scholar, we could offer a full-day program like Summer Advantage's, one designed to meet scholars' intellectual needs and build their confidence (and I knew that, yes, we could make it fun for the scholars). The program was an overwhelming success.

Soon, David, Ethan, and Kay at the Mind Trust and some Indiana government leaders encouraged me to apply for a charter for a school of my own. It wasn't a challenge I would have taken earlier on in my career, but I understood how powerful it could be to build our own institutions, literally.

I wasn't quite sure how to move forward, though, and I turned to my girlfriend at the time, Terra, for advice. Terra had been a Wall Street lawyer, but after multiple firms tried to use her as free networking to recruit Black talent, she left to create her own profitable Diversity, Equity, and Inclusion business. She was soft-spoken and buoyant, but she was used to breaking her own ground. She sympathized with my years of struggles with big philanthropic interests, and she understood that I still wanted to reach far beyond education.

"Earl," she told me one night, over our own kitchen table, "you need to find a way to work independently."

She explained to me how we could build an umbrella company that would serve as the foundation for our schools, and for any other projects we might choose to take on. By budgeting and planning carefully, we could build schools using public funds alone, reducing our dependence on private money. I saw the vision I'd had for years, reflected back at me more clearly than ever. It was time to get to work.

I assembled a small team, and we found an old, empty Cadillac dealership near Fall Creek, in Indianapolis. With $2.5 million in renovations, it became our first school. Of course, I always knew what we would name it: George and Veronica Phalen Leadership Academy.

Sunday Mornings

I never stopped having Sunday breakfast with my parents. Every week, they knew to expect me at the table. I'd keep my mom company in the kitchen and set the plates out; after breakfast, we'd sit together with our drinks and talk about the week ahead. They always wanted to hear about what was going on at work. No detail was too boring or too technical. We loved, shared, and sometimes sparred over the years, but that kitchen table never stopped being a place for debate. Most importantly, it never stopped being my center and my place for unconditional love.

In the winter of 2007, my dad started to slow down. He was a man of his time, a World War II veteran who didn't believe in coddling or complaints. Every week, I would see him, calm and stoic as ever, taking a little longer to get out of his chair, pausing on the trip from the kitchen to the living room. For six months, he was with us, but fading. We lost him in June of 2008, and my world faded too.

Those first few months of grief were very hard. I was lucky to have my family close. I started seeing my mom twice a week. We comforted each other, remembered my dad together. When I wasn't with my mom, I just sat on the couch in my condo in my sweatpants, watching the kind of TV shows I'd always thought were a waste of time. I'd melt into my seat for hours of *Jerry Springer*, *Steve Wilkos*, and *Maury*, get up, sit down, watch *Monk* and *Walker, Texas Ranger* marathons, eat takeout, repeat. Without my dad's guiding light, the way ahead just seemed drab and dark. I didn't want to do anything. It wasn't like me to lie around, but I was stuck with questions that seemed to have no answer. How could I find the energy for the work ahead? What do I do when a loss has no silver lining, no secret higher purpose? It took about six months, but one day I was lying on the sofa and it was like I heard my dad's voice in my head. *Earl*, I imagined him saying. *This is not who you are. It's time to get back at it.* And I did, knowing a part of him would always be with me. I don't think it's an accident that the call from Motty, and the next chapter of my career, came soon afterward.

I was blessed to have so many beautiful moments with my mom for another eleven years. She left us just before Christmas, in 2019, and I miss her every day. When we were younger, no matter how big and far-flung the Phalen family got, we always had Thanksgiving and Christmas at my parents', Jimmy's big birthday party for my mom in July, and summer days at the beach house. My parents always wanted the family to keep coming together, even after they were gone; in their later years, they started handing down their holiday traditions to the next generation. My parents asked me to host the Christmas get-together. Now, I am blessed to see my family and my incredible nieces and nephews at least once a year for an afternoon full of love, reconnection, and positive energy.

I see reflections of Mom and Dad in all of us. It's been an honor to have the love and support of my siblings as PLA continues its journey. Jimmy serves as chair of my board, and he and Rosemary have made major donations to the organization over the years. David helps us with legal matters, and Steve sometimes lends us his financial expertise. Joanie, Patty, and Ann are in related fields—

Joanie as an educator and counselor, Patty as a teacher with a focus on career-oriented technical education, and Ann as a devoted special education teacher—and I learn so much from each of them. Mary allows me to call or text her—the way I used to reach out to my mom—any time something positive happens for PLA.

When I was putting together PLA's statement of values, I decided to interview all of my family members about what they thought our core values should be. The same five messages came up, over and over again. Children come first, always. We should be grateful that we get to serve. Respect is fundamental. Determination: if you want something, you have to work hard for it. And I think the one that underlies all of these values, the one that spurs me to keep going in good and bad times, is my parents' philosophy of continuous improvement. They loved us unconditionally, and that love helped us reach to become better and better versions of ourselves. Whenever I showed off a new golf swing or my latest report card to my dad, he had his old saying ready: "It's good, but there's room for improvement." I knew both my parents believed there was no limit to what we kids could achieve. Eventually, I came to believe it too.

Closure

I carry the legacy of my birth family with me as well. It's a more complicated inheritance, and one that took me time to come to peace with. I had been curious about meeting my birth mother since I was a teenager. I had spent nine months growing inside of her, completely dependent on her, and completely enveloped by her. There had to be a connection there. There were times I shied away from searching for her. I would get ready to make a call to the agency, then talk myself out of it at the last minute. But in my twenties, I talked with a friend, a Black woman my age who had also been adopted by a white family. She told me that meeting her birth mother had "closed a hole in her heart." I needed to know if I would feel the same way.

I found my birth mother several years later, in my mid-thirties. We spoke on the phone first. She told me the story of her own childhood—a cold and neglectful mother who wouldn't speak to her, followed by eight years in the house of a strict but loving aunt. She had had a boyfriend who left for Vietnam and came back a shell of his former self, no longer interested in a future with her or with anyone. Heartbroken and confused, she went out with another man and got pregnant. She and my birth father weren't ready for a child. They were young, and they hardly knew each other. Her aunt had been staunchly against abortion. She had given birth to me, held me for those thirty minutes in the hospital, and then gone back to North Carolina to move on with her life.

I met my birth father as well, soon after my mother's call. As it turned out, he had been a truck driver in the Eastern Corridor for the past twenty years, and he had often made deliveries to a grocery store in Norwood, just five minutes from where I grew up. We might have seen each other there when I was a kid. After our first conversation, we talked on the phone for a few months before deciding to meet up when his route took him through Massachusetts.

On a winter day in 2002, I sat across from him in a Dunkin' Donuts and scanned his face, looking for signs of my connection to the man who had given me life. I didn't see much of a resemblance between us, and my birth father must not have either: the first thing he told me was that I looked just like my mother. We talked about his life on the road, his vacation plans, another son of his who lived in Florida and shared his first name. After that polite but stilted meeting, my birth father and I didn't talk much. I think he had been looking for something, and he didn't find it. I don't know if I was looking for anything at all. I am grateful to him for the bond I came to share with my grandmom, whose courage and fierce, protective love I feel proud to carry inside me.

As for my birth mom, we took it slow, and over the years, we developed a warm relationship. Hearing her story, and seeing her face, put some unanswered questions to rest. When I met my younger biological brother, Nate, I was surprised and inspired to learn that he has his own nonprofit, too, helping incarcerated people lead financially healthy lives. It's been a blessing to have him and his wife, Cathy, in my life—even if it means I'm not quite the youngest child anymore.

I never went back to the therapist who I talked to about my adoption trauma, the feelings of abandonment I acted out in my relationships with women. Her words stuck with me, but they didn't alter my path. I have some regrets, but intimacy is a puzzle it can take a lifetime to solve. Over the years, I've come to understand that my journey has given me a unique insight into the complexities of human connection. My parents didn't give me life, but I can't imagine the story of my life without them. I have struggled many times with feeling alone and unheard, and yet my greatest accomplishment as a leader has been finding and keeping the wonderful people I work with. I am not a biological father, but I have been privileged to watch generations of children learn and grow under BELL's and PLA's care. A life committed to service has given me more than I ever thought possible. And it's been a long time since I felt the loneliness that followed me when I was younger, the sense that few understood my secret inner world. As an adult, I've found strength and inspiration in my connections with my closest friends, with family, and with men who have walked similar paths. For the past fourteen years, I've met once a month with a group of other Black men—David, Adam, Michael, and Emmett. We all show up at one of our houses for a few hours of fellowship, a time when we can talk and joke about whatever's on our minds and share the challenges of our lives, freely and confidentially. That feeling of true brotherhood has been hard earned, and it has meant so much to me. I'm grateful to my old mentor Hubie for bringing us together. If there was ever a hole in my heart, it found a way to mend itself.

Lessons in Leadership

As Tom Clancy once said, "an overnight success is ten years in the making." In our case, it was more like seventeen years. Over a decade of trial and error at BELL helped us hit the ground running at PLA. We opened our first school in Indiana in 2013. By 2015, we had two academies; we added three more in 2016, another three in 2017, and by 2021, there were twenty-four Phalen Leadership Academies in Alabama, Indiana, Michigan, Ohio, Texas, and Washington, DC. We don't always build from the ground up, like we did with the first Phalen Leadership Academy. In Indianapolis, I was fortunate to partner with and learn from Nicole Fama, an expert in school turnarounds. We also got to work with her amazing father, Bill, who we and hundreds of students fondly call "Coach." With Nicole's leadership, dedication, and programmatic and logistical expertise, and the fundraising and organizational development skills I built at BELL, we were able to start making the quick, lasting improvements so many schools desperately need. And when we were building that first school, I had the advice and support of my girlfriend, Katina, who had spent nine years as a special educator in some of Indianapolis's most underserved schools. She and her school-aged daughter Lizzy were there with me, bringing life into my plans to for the building, helping me understand how we could give the children of Indianapolis the same unconditional love and high standards my parents gave me.

I'm still proud that throughout my career, I have always had a team of great people. Some of the team have been with us from the beginning, and others have moved on or joined later; all have been crucial to our success. In those early years and beyond, I was and am so lucky to work with Eva, who inspires unconditional trust and excellence; Katina, who brought a true teacher's perspective to our work; Andrea, who had developed a brilliant model and quality assurance process; Michelle, whose honesty was a guiding light; Amber, who can take on any task and make it happen; Nicole (Scott), whose calm and legal skills helps lead us through storms; Johnny, a strategist and federal grant genius who ensures we have the resources to bring our aggressive plans to life; and Natasha, who balances a huge array of projects with flexibility and grace.

We've transformed ten F and D-performing schools into A and B-rated schools, in just a few years. At the end of my first eleven years at BELL, we had a $2 million budget and were able to serve 2,000 students. In seven years, we've built PLA into an $118 million nonprofit, with 1,096 team members who impact the lives of 10,000 children. *It's good, but there's room for improvement.*

When you're young, you rebel against your parents. Sometimes getting older and wiser means realizing all the times they were right. I used to get angry at my father for trying to bring his banker's perspective to the work of running a nonprofit. Now, I understand how many of my wisest leadership decisions come from his voice in the back of my mind.

Keep your expenses lower than your revenues—I internalized that one eventually. Fundraising is still a challenging game, full of political minefields, but I've learned to be ambitious rather than reckless. My dad would always tell me to "keep it lean," and it wasn't until I was a few years in at BELL until I saw what he meant. In the early days, we used to staff summer classrooms with one teacher and two student TAs, to keep the student-to-teacher ratio low. It never worked the way we hoped: one or the other TA was always standing around with nothing to do, and the teacher had an extra headache trying to manage and make work for them both. The scholars didn't get better attention or instruction. We dropped to one teacher and one TA, saved money, and made everyone happier—and our program was significantly better. I know now that there's a difference between maintaining a growth mindset and acting as if more is always better. And I don't hide from bad news anymore—I channel my father's pragmatism and address our challenges head-on.

And when I struggle to lead, I remember my mother's empathy, the way she saw the good in everyone. My mother really saw people—she took the time to listen to them and understand them, and she earned their lifelong trust as a result. I work every day to extend that same understanding to others—I'm not even close to her level, but the effort is worth making. My mother was firm in her principles, but she didn't close herself off from other people; she found her purpose in helping and connecting with others. Her example reminds me that my job as a leader is to find other leaders and support them. I can give that support, because of the way she once gave it to me. And I know if I'm ever lost, I have the memories of all those Sunday mornings, the wisdom, and the care I got at that table from my mother and my father.

The Future

I'm a steadier, slightly more calculated CEO now. Even so, I don't regret all the risks I took in those early years of BELL. The need is still so great. One in five American children of color still lives in poverty. Five million of our children attend failing schools today. When you see someone drowning, you don't turn around and go sign up for lifeguard training. You jump in the water. Ever since that day in Jamaica, I've known that I was called to help children learn. But I believed in service before I was an educator, and when I see the neighborhoods, our schools are in now, I remember why I felt called to write a master plan over twenty years ago. Our scholars face obstacles that no child should have to tackle. When my great-great-grandfather was a young man during Reconstruction, he opened his own grocery store rather than pay triple prices in white-owned businesses that made him walk through the back door. Today, many of our scholars live in communities without any grocery stores at all. They have to walk to the gas station on roads without sidewalks, to places where they can't buy fresh fruit and are charged double for basic staples.

I think of scholars like TaeVeon, who lives in an apartment building in Indianapolis. She stopped waiting for the bus in the morning and started waking up early and sprinting the two miles to school. When her teacher asked her why she ran, she told her that there had been a shooting in her building, a quadruple homicide. She knew if she stood still, she'd be an easier target.

We never stop pushing for more, for better, for our scholars and our communities. In 2020, in the wake of George Floyd's murder, we launched PLA University. The university offers tuition-free professional skills workshops and credential programs for the adult relatives of our PLA scholars. With professional training, the more than 100,000 family members who make up our PLA community can secure jobs paying over $40,000 a year. Inside our schools, our Summer Advantage and Reading Advantage programs offer extra support to scholars both during and outside the school year. PLA's Arts & Cultural center is the only one of its kind on Indy's Far Eastside, and we're proud to offer state-of-the-art recording equipment and culturally responsive art to thousands of children. I'm especially excited for the launch of the Sean Cowdrey Complex, which will host health and wellness programs as well as youth sports leagues and adult fitness programs including yoga, dance, and weight training. Our expansion is what I've dreamed about for so many years, and it's a dream I feel humbled to share with so many people in the PLA community. As for me, I haven't stopped growing either. I still push myself hard. I think ambitious people never get rid of that feeling of *not enough*. Not enough time, not enough reach, not enough change. The difference is, I don't have that doubt deep inside that I don't belong, that I wasn't meant to lead. I may never feel that I've done enough, but I know now that I *am* enough. And I want all of our scholars to know it too. I want them to understand that they're unstoppable. I want to create a world where there's nothing in their way.

Calling the Shots

I call the Phalen Falcons basketball team in for a huddle. We've played this team once before—and we lost. Tonight, is different. We're in the fourth quarter, and neither team has maintained more than a five-point lead. While the score is high, the ball has been turned over ten times. The crowd at the gym is growing excited, rowdy even. It's down to the wire.

I look at Curtis, one of my best defenders, and Keith, a point guard with sharp ballhandling skills.

"You know they're going to pass it to number 14," I tell them. "Curtis, really stick tight, and Keith, you come help him."

They pass it to #14, and Curtis cuts him off on the left. Same thing on the right. Finally, #14 passes it away to the wing and makes a hard move to the basket. Pushing Curtis off with his left hand, he creates just enough space to get a return pass and get off an eight-footer.

I'm in agony, running back and forth on the sidelines, willing the ball not to go in.

Swish.

They're up by one, with six seconds to go.

"Time out!" my players yell together, hustling back to the sidelines for one last chance to plan a victory.

I come to our games straight from work, sitting on a dingy folded chair in suit pants and a vest, and dress shirt with the top button undone. By the end of the game, I've sweated through my button-down and my pleated slacks, and my voice is hoarse from cheering—my players might call it hysterical yelling—on the sidelines. I will say that in all my time as a coach, I have never received a technical foul. Have I been pulled aside and spoken to by one or two refs? No comment.

I'm a pretty passionate person, but I hold myself back about 95 percent of the time—in the boardroom, and sometimes as a leader. On the basketball court, in practices and at games, I am free. I am my truest, most uninhibited self. The players appreciate the commitment. I don't run as fast or jump as high as I used to, and the team thinks it's hilarious when I'm straining to keep up during our practice scrimmages. But I surprise them sometimes: I haven't taught them all of my tricks yet. I can still execute a pick-and-roll that they don't see coming. And I know how to push off to create space.

Being with the team is about more than sports: it's support, its mentorship, it's hands-on learning. It's something I know I'll do long after I retire. I watch the players learn to lift each other up, take ownership of their choices. Even as they grow into independent young men, they know they can come to me with any problem, large or small. I know how important it is to have those role models. I never want them to hold back.

One of my co-MVPs, Eric, is leading the huddle. Suddenly, Jay speaks up. He's usually comfortable deferring to Eric on the last play, but the look in his eyes tells me he's ready to make a bold move.

"I want the ball," Jay tells the team. "Curtis, you pass it in. I'll get open. I don't care how covered I might seem, throw it in my direction and I'll come up with it."

"The rest of you," he says to Eric, Dalon, Curtis, and Keith, "just give me room. I'll get the shot."

The Falcons look at each other with unspoken trust.

"OK," Curtis says. Time in.

Five. Jay catches the ball and starts driving it down the court to the left. He dodges one defender and has to cross over to avoid another.

Four. A quick crossover dribble has him headed straight down the center of the court again. I clench my fists, almost afraid to watch, but knowing I can trust the determination in his eyes. The players on the bench—Alex, Shamar, Jamie, Marquis, Darrance, and Tim—are just as riveted as I am, yelling encouragement at their friends and teammates.

Three. He makes it to the free throw line. #14 tries to block him, but Jay goes strong into his chest and gets some distance.

Two. No hesitation whatsoever. The ball just flows off his fingertips.

One.

"Yes!" I screamed.

"Yes!!!" I hear the Falcons jumping on the court. The players on the bench get out of their seats, and so does the crowd. The echoes of victory ring around the gym's domed ceiling.

He made it. We made it. We won.

AFTERWORD

This book was a labor of love that I have been blessed to complete with the support of so many along the way. Thank you!

I also want to share that the Ewing Marion Kauffman Foundation has also been a consistent presence and support on this journey. Since the writing of this book, I have been blessed to join KC Scholars as its CEO and President and together, we will continue to exemplify Mr. Kauffman's vision and belief that everyone has a fundamental right to quality education that transforms their life.

Since its inception, KC Scholars has awarded 6,069 scholarships of $50,000 each to high students in Kansas City. Scholars have achieved 94% annual persistence rates and are on track for 75% graduation rates, which is 7 times the national average for first-generation, low-income students.

We also recently launched a program for adults, 18 and older, who are currently earning under $45,000 per year. Both my mother and father would be proud of our newest program, which prayerfully will help 50,000 adults secure jobs that enable them to care for themselves and their loved ones.

As the spirit of my parents continues to guide me, I am grateful for the many places it has led me. Their story and my story is one of love, resilience, and belief that we are all children of Jesus and deserve to be our best selves.

ABOUT THE AUTHOR

Earl Martin Phalen is one of K-12 education's most visionary leaders: a founder and CEO of multiple successful nonprofits, his mission is to deliver educational excellence and equity to low-income Black and brown children. Born into the Massachusetts foster care system, Earl was adopted into a large, loving Irish Catholic family at age two. His parents instilled the values that led him to a life of service, but growing up Black in a largely white, often hostile world made it hard for him to embrace his gifts. Earl's education taught him the power of Black self-determination, and the love of his family and community sustained him as he struggled to become the leader he'd once doubted he could be. Earl's exciting career is a testament to his mission's core message: all children deserve the support, the opportunity, and the self-belief they need to reach for their dreams without hesitation. He currently resides in Quincy, MA.

ABOUT THE BOOK

As a black boy adopted into a large, loving Irish Catholic family at age two, Earl discovered at a young age that he was meant to stand out. Yet whether it was on the basketball court or early in his career as a young and ambitious "edupreneur," Earl encountered opportunities that required him to give his all, but often found himself holding back. Earl faced both subtle and overt racism in his predominantly white neighborhoods, but with the love and unrelenting support of his family, he was able to overcome much—facing it most directly and intentionally for the first time when he arrived on Yale campus as a young athlete scholar. While at Yale, Earl gained a new sense of pride and purpose as he connected with his black and African American heritage. This would continue throughout his studies and into graduate school at Harvard Law, where his calling to education—particularly that of black and brown children—came to life. Earl has dedicated his life to improving the access poor, black and brown children have to quality education and opportunities.

A free ebook edition is available with the purchase of this book.

To claim your free ebook edition:

1. Visit MorganJamesBOGO.com
2. Sign your name CLEARLY in the space
3. Complete the form and submit a photo of the entire copyright page
4. You or your friend can download the ebook to your preferred device

Morgan James BOGO™

A **FREE** ebook edition is available for you or a friend with the purchase of this print book.

_____

CLEARLY SIGN YOUR NAME ABOVE

Instructions to claim your free ebook edition:
1. Visit MorganJamesBOGO.com
2. Sign your name CLEARLY in the space above
3. Complete the form and submit a photo of this entire page
4. You or your friend can download the ebook to your preferred device

Print & Digital Together Forever.

Snap a photo

Free ebook

Read anywhere